THE
COMING TO
AMERICA
COOKBOOK

THE COMING TO AMERICA COOKBOOK

DELICIOUS RECIPES AND FASCINATING STORIES FROM AMERICA'S MANY CULTURES

Joan D'Amico

Karen Eich Drummond, Ed.D., R.D.

Illustrations by Lizzy Rockwell
and Tina Cash-Walsh

WILEY

John Wiley & Sons, Inc.

Published by John Wiley & Sons, Inc., Hoboken, New Jersey
Published simultaneously in Canada

Design and composition by Navta Associates, Inc.

The publisher and the authors have made every reasonable effort to ensure that the experiments and activities in this book are safe when conducted as instructed but assume no responsibility for any damage caused or sustained while performing the experiments or activities in the book. Parents, guardians, and/or teachers should supervise young readers who undertake the experiments and activities in this book.

For general information about our other products and services, please contact our Customer Care Department within the United States at (800) 762-2974, outside the United States at (317) 572-3993 or fax (317) 572-4002.

Wiley also publishes its books in a variety of electronic formats. Some content that appears in print may not be available in electronic books. For more information about Wiley products, visit our web site at www.wiley.com.

Library of Congress Cataloging-in-Publication Data

D'Amico, Joan, date.
  The coming to America cookbook : delicious recipes and fascinating stories from America's many cultures / Joan D'Amico and Karen Eich Drummond.
      p.   cm.
   ISBN 0-471-48335-4 (pbk.)
1. Cookery, International—Juvenile literature. 2. Cookery—United States—Juvenile literature. I. Drummond, Karen Eich. II. Title.
   TX725.A1D25 2005
   641.59—dc22
2004014947

Printed in the United States of America

10 9 8 7 6 5 4 3 2 1

To my budding author, Caitlin Drummond—and her family and ancestors from Scotland, Germany, England, and the Netherlands.

And to the D'Amico children, Christi, Alexa, and Kyle— and their ancestors from Italy, Germany, England, and Ireland.

CONTENTS

# ABOUT THIS BOOK

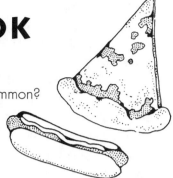

Do you know what these foods have in common?

- Pizza
- Frankfurters
- Fried rice
- Burritos

They are all popular American foods that were originally brought to America by immigrants from other countries: pizza from Italy, frankfurters from Germany, fried rice from Asia, and burritos from Mexico. Of course, many dishes that immigrants brought to America have been changed, often because different ingredients are available here.

Every American other than Native Americans is either an immigrant or related to one. An immigrant is someone who enters a new country to live. Over the last few centuries, millions of immigrants have made their way to America—and hundreds of thousands still come each year. Some, like slaves, came unwillingly. Many immigrants who came to America were drawn by the promise of a better life—the chance to get a job, for instance, or land to farm and build a home. Others came to this country to escape religious persecution, wars, and political unrest.

The United States has had four major waves of immigrants. The first wave began with the early colonists and reached a peak just before the Revolutionary War broke out in 1775. During the first wave, most of the immigrants came from England, Scotland, Germany, Ireland, and Italy. The second wave of immigration lasted from the 1820s to the 1870s. About a third of these immigrants were Irish escaping the potato famine. The largest wave of immigrants came to America from the 1880s to the early 1920s. Over 20 million people traveled from every corner of the world. During this period, more and more Americans began to see the flood of immigrants as a threat to their jobs and the nation's unity. In the 1920s, the United States put into effect immigration laws that allowed only a set number of immigrants from each country each year. Europeans were favored over Asians and Africans. Only 1,000 people were allowed each year from all of Asia and Africa. The fourth and continuing wave of immigrants began in 1965, when changes in the immigration laws eliminated the country of origin as a basis for immigration to the United States.

During colonial times, most immigrants arrived in Philadelphia, the major colonial port. During the early 1800s, New York City began to replace Philadelphia as the chief port of entry for immigrants. Between 1892 and 1954, over 12 million immigrants saw the Statue of Liberty in New York Harbor before getting off boats and entering the Ellis Island immigration station. On Ellis Island, all immigrants were checked for disease and disability before being registered and then completing their long journeys. The Ellis Island facility has been restored and is now open as a museum. You can use their Web site to see if one of your ancestors passed through there (www.ellisisland.org). Over 100 million Americans are related to someone who came to America through Ellis Island.

Immigrants came to America from many different countries and cultures, and every group has its own favorite foods and eating habits. For example, Mexican *cuisine*, or the food that is prepared by a particular group, is going to be different from the cuisine of Moroccans from North Africa. These countries have different landscapes and climates, which influence what types of crops and livestock can be raised. Different religions are practiced in these countries, and religion often affects what people eat. For example, pork is not eaten in Morocco because most Moroccans are Muslim. Every country also has a unique history that influences what people eat today. For example, when the Spaniards took over Mexico, they introduced Mexicans to beef, pork, chicken, wheat, and apples. Another factor that influences what people eat is the amount of money available to buy or grow food. In poorer countries such as Ethiopia, meatless stews are very common and are an economical way to feed a big family.

Before you start cooking the recipes in this book, be sure to read the "Discovering the Kitchen" section. It covers the basics on kitchen safety, utensils, cooking terms, and measuring. Each recipe lists how much time you will need to make it, the kitchen tools you'll need, and the number of servings it makes.

From arroz con pollo, a Spanish dish of rice with chicken, to wat, a peppery stew eaten in Ethiopia, we know you'll appreciate the diversity and the cooking traditions of the immigrants who have contributed to the American "salad bowl" and made American cooking so exciting. Have fun learning about food and culture in twenty countries, and *bon appétit*, a French expression meaning "enjoy your meal"!

DISCOVERING THE KITCHEN

Tools of the Trade

baking pan

colander

cutting board

biscuit cutter

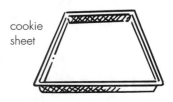

cookie sheet

electric blender

grater

Let's take a close look at the cooking equipment in your kitchen. These are the basic tools you'll need to prepare the recipes in this book. Any kitchen tools that are used in only one or two recipes are described within those recipes.

baking pan   A square or rectangular pan used for baking and cooking foods in the oven. The most common sizes are 9 × 13-inch and 8-inch square.

biscuit cutter   A round outline, usually made from metal, used to cut biscuits from dough.

colander   A large perforated bowl used for rinsing food and draining pasta or other foods.

cookie sheet   A large rectangular pan with no sides or with one-inch sides, used for baking cookies and other foods.

cutting board   Made from wood or plastic, cutting boards provide a surface on which to cut foods.

egg separator   A small, shallow cup with slots used to separate the egg whites from the yolk. The yolk sits in the middle while the whites drop through the slots into a bowl.

electric blender   A glass or plastic cylinder with a rotating blade at the bottom. A small motor in the base turns the blade. The blender has different speeds and is used for mixing, blending, grinding, and pureeing.

grater   A metal surface with sharp-edged holes used for shredding and grating foods such as vegetables and cheese.

hand-held electric mixer Two beaters that rotate to mix ingredients together. Used for mashed potatoes, cake batters, and other mixing jobs.

knives:

- **paring knife** A knife with a small pointed blade used for trimming and paring vegetables and fruits and other cutting jobs that don't require a larger knife. (Most recipes in this book call for a knife. You will find the paring knife works well in most situations.)

- **peeler** A hand-held tool that removes the peel from fruits and vegetables.

- **sandwich spreader** A knife with a dull blade that is designed to spread fillings on bread.

- **table knife** A knife used as a utensil at the table.

layer cake pans Round metal pans used to bake layers of a cake.

measuring cups Cups with measurements (½ cup, ⅓ cup, etc.) on the side, bottom, or handle. Measuring cups that have spouts are used for liquid ingredients. Measuring cups without spouts are used for dry ingredients such as flour.

measuring spoons Used for measuring small amounts of foods such as spices. They come in a set of 1 tablespoon, 1 teaspoon, ½ teaspoon, and ¼ teaspoon.

microwave-safe dish A dish that can safely be used in the microwave oven. The best microwave dishes say "microwave safe" on the label. Don't use metal pans, aluminum foil, plastic foam containers, brown paper bags, plastic wrap, or margarine tubs in the microwave.

mixing bowls Round-bottomed bowls used for mixing and whipping all kinds of foods. Depending on the amount of ingredients, a large, medium, or small bowl may be used.

muffin tins Metal or glass pans with small, round cups used for baking muffins and cupcakes.

hand-held electric mixer

paring knife

sandwich spreader

layer cake pan

measuring cup

measuring spoons

mixing bowl

muffin tin

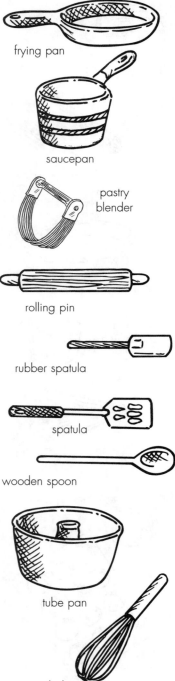

frying pan

saucepan

pastry blender

rolling pin

rubber spatula

spatula

wooden spoon

tube pan

whisk

pans:

- **frying pan** (also called a sauté pan)   Used for cooking foods, such as hamburgers or onions, in hot fat.

- **saucepan** (also called a pot)   Used for general stovetop cooking, such as boiling pasta or simmering a sauce.

pastry blender   A group of stiff wires attached to both ends of a handle. It is used, with a rocking motion, to blend butter or margarine into flour and other dry ingredients to make a dough.

rolling pin   A wooden or plastic roller used to flatten items such as piecrust and biscuit dough.

rubber spatula   A flat, flexible rubber or plastic tip on a long handle. It is used to scrape bowls, pots, and pans and for **folding** (a gentle over-and-under motion) ingredients into whipped cream or other whipped batter.

spatula   A flat metal or plastic tool used for lifting and turning meats, eggs, and other foods.

spoons:

- **teaspoon**   A spoon used for measuring. Also the name for the spoon normally used as a utensil at the table.

- **wooden spoon**   Used for mixing ingredients together and stirring.

tube pan   A metal cake pan with a center tube used for making angel food cakes, Bundt cakes, and special breads.

whisk   Used especially for whipping egg whites and cream.

wire rack   Used for cooling baked goods.

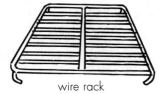

wire rack

Cooking Skills

Chefs need to master cutting and measuring skills and the basics of mixing and stovetop cooking. Here are the skills you will be practicing as you try the recipes in this book.

CUTTING

Foods are cut before cooking so that they will look good and cook evenly. Place the food to be cut on a cutting board and use a knife that is a comfortable size for your hand. To hold the knife, place your hand on top of the handle and fit your fingers around the handle. The grip should be secure but relaxed. In your other hand, hold the item being cut. Keep your fingertips curled under to protect them from cuts. (See the "Safety Rules" section on page 11 for more on how to cut safely.)

Here are some commonly used cutting terms you'll need to know:

chop   To cut into irregularly shaped pieces.

dice   To cut into cubes of the same size.

mince   To chop very fine.

slice   To cut into uniform slices.

Grating and shredding are also examples of cutting:

grate   To rub a food across a grater's tiny punched holes to produce small or fine pieces of food. Hard cheeses and some vegetables are grated.

shred   To rub a food across a surface with medium to large holes or slits. Shredded foods look like strips. The cheese used for making pizza is always shredded.

chopped

diced

minced

sliced

grate

shred

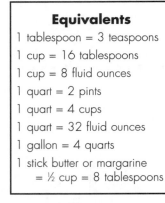

liquid
measurement

dry
measurement

beat

fold

whip

MEASURING

Ingredients can be measured in three different ways: by counting (six apples), by measuring volume (½ cup of applesauce), or by measuring weight (a pound of apples).

To measure the volume of a liquid, always place the measuring cup on a flat surface and check that the liquid goes up to the proper line on the measuring cup while you are looking directly at it at eye level.

To measure the volume of a dry ingredient, such as flour, spoon it into the measuring cup and level it off with a table knife. Do not pack the cup with the dry ingredient—that is, don't press down on it to make room for more—unless the recipe says to.

MIXING

There are all kinds of ways to mix! Here are definitions of the most common types.

beat   To move a utensil back and forth to blend ingredients together.

cream   To mix a solid fat (usually margarine or butter) and sugar by pressing them against a bowl with the back of a spoon until they look creamy.

fold   To move a utensil with a gentle over-and-under motion.

mix   To combine ingredients so that they are all evenly distributed.

whip   To beat rapidly using a circular motion, usually with a whisk, to incorporate air into the mixture (such as in making whipped cream).

whisk   To beat ingredients together lightly with a wire whisk until they are well blended.

STOVETOP COOKING

There are different ways to cook on your stove. Here are descriptions of cooking methods you will be practicing as you try the recipes in this book. Because it is easy to get burned while cooking on the stove, see the "Safety Rules" section on page 11.

boil   To heat a liquid to its boiling point, or to cook in a boiling liquid. Water boils at 212°F. You can tell it is boiling when you see lots of large bubbles popping to the surface. When a liquid boils, it is turning into steam (the gaseous state of water). Water can't get any hotter than 212°F; it can only make steam faster. Boiling is most often used for cooking pasta.

panfry   To cook in a pan over moderate heat in a small amount of fat. Hamburgers are an example of a food that can be panfried.

sauté   To cook quickly in a pan over medium-high heat in a small amount of fat. Vegetables, especially onions, are often sautéed in oil to bring out their flavor and brown them.

simmer   To heat a liquid to just below its boiling point, or to cook in a simmering liquid. You can tell a liquid is simmering when it has bubbles floating slowly to the surface. Most foods cooked in liquid are simmered. Always watch simmering foods closely so that they do not boil.

steam   To cook in steam. Steam has much more heat and cooks foods more quickly than boiling water does. Steaming is an excellent method for cooking most vegetables.

boil

sauté

simmer

CRACKING AND SEPARATING EGGS

It is best to crack an egg into a clear glass cup (such as a measuring cup) before adding it to the other ingredients. That way, if the egg smells bad or has a red spot, you can throw it out before the egg goes in with the other ingredients. An egg with a red spot is safe to eat but is usually thrown out because of its appearance. You should also remove any pieces of eggshell from the egg before adding the egg to the other ingredients.

Sometimes you will need to separate the egg yolk from the egg white for a recipe. To do this, crack the egg over an egg separator and a bowl. Make sure you get the yolk in the middle. The whites will drain out into the bowl. If you don't have an egg separator, you can separate an egg by cracking it over a bowl, keeping the yolk in one-half of the shell. Carefully pass the egg yolk from one-half of the shell to the other without letting it break until the white has fallen into the bowl.

SAFETY RULES

The kitchen can be a safe, or a very dangerous, part of your home. What's dangerous in your kitchen? Sharp knives, boiling water, and hot oil are a few things. Always check with an adult before trying any of the recipes. Talk to him or her about what you are allowed to do by yourself and when you need an adult's assistance. And always follow these safety guidelines.

AROUND THE STOVE AND OVEN

- Get an adult's permission before you use a stove or oven.
- Don't wear long, baggy shirts or sweaters when cooking. They could catch fire.
- Never turn your back on a frying pan that contains oil.
- Never fry with oil at a high temperature.
- Don't spray a pan with vegetable oil cooking spray over the stove or near heat. Oil will burn at high temperatures, so spray the pan over the sink.
- If a fire starts in a pan on the stove, you can smother it by covering it with the pan lid or pouring baking soda on it. Never use water to put out a fire in a pan with oil—it only makes a fire worse.
- Always use pot holders or wear oven mitts when using the oven or handling something that is hot. Make sure your pot holders are not wet. Wet pot holders transmit the heat from the hot item you are holding directly to your skin.
- Don't overfill pans with boiling or simmering liquids.
- Open pan lids away from you to let steam escape safely.

- Keep pan handles turned away from the edge of the stove. Knocking against them can splatter hot food.
- Stir foods with long-handled spoons.
- Keep pets and small children away from hot stoves and ovens during cooking. (Try to keep them out of the kitchen altogether.)

USING ANY APPLIANCE

- Use an appliance only if you know exactly how to operate it and you have permission from an adult.
- Never operate an appliance that is near the sink or sitting in water.
- Don't use frayed electrical cords or damaged plugs and outlets. Tell an adult.

USING A MICROWAVE OVEN

- Use only microwave-safe cookware, paper towels, paper plates, or paper cups.
- Use pot holders or oven mitts to remove items.
- If a dish is covered, make sure there is some opening through which steam can escape during cooking.
- When taking foods out of the microwave, you must open the container so that steam escapes *away* from your hands and face.
- Prick foods like potatoes and hot dogs with a fork before putting them into the microwave.
- Never try to cook a whole egg in the microwave—it will burst!

USING A KNIFE

- Get an adult's permission before using any knife.
- Always pick up a knife by its handle.
- Pay attention to what you're doing!
- Cut away from the body and away from anyone near you.
- Use a sliding, back-and-forth motion when slicing foods with a knife.
- Don't leave a knife near the edge of a table. It can be easily knocked off, or a small child may touch it.
- Don't try to catch a falling knife.
- Don't use knives to cut string, to open cans or bottles, or as a screwdriver.
- Don't put a knife into a sink full of water. Instead, put it on the drainboard, to avoid cutting yourself.

CLEANING UP

Whenever you use a knife and cutting board to cut meat, poultry, or seafood, be sure to wash them thoroughly before using them again. These foods contain germs that can be harmful, and you don't want the germs to get onto foods that won't be cooked, such as vegetables for salads.

CHAPTER 1

BRAZIL

Shaped like a diamond, Brazil lies in the heart of South America. Brazil borders ten countries. In South America, only Ecuador and Chile do not border Brazil. Brazil's coastline along the Atlantic Ocean extends for over 4,500 miles. Northern Brazil is home to the Amazon rain forest, a hot and wet region on the Amazon River. Plains, plateaus, and mountains occupy the rest of the country. Warm tropical weather extends north from Rio de Janeiro (the capital) throughout most of the year. South of Rio de Janeiro, the climate generally includes warm summers and cold winters.

Brazil was home to millions of native Brazilians for thousands of years before a Portuguese sailor, Pedro Alvares Cabral, landed there in 1500. Cabral was trying to reach India to trade for spices, silk, and other valuables. Instead, he claimed the region for Portugal. Portuguese colonists started moving to coastal sections of Brazil, and many planted sugarcane. Between 1550 and 1850, about 4 million Africans were brought as slaves to Brazil to work in the sugarcane fields. Later, farmers grew coffee, which continues today to be a very important crop. In 1822, Brazil declared its independence from Portugal, but the national language is still Portuguese.

For most of the 1900s, Brazil welcomed immigrants from around the world. In the past 40 years, however, Brazilians have been emigrating to the United States and other countries because of Brazil's growing population, which has led to overcrowded cities and a poor economy. Many immigrants came to the United States looking for better-paying jobs and settled in cities such as New York and Boston.

Brazilian culture and foods reflect the four major groups of people who make up the population of Brazil: native Brazilians, Portuguese and other Europeans, Africans, and Asians. The **samba** is a famous Brazilian dance with African origins. The **bossa nova** is a popular Brazilian music that combines jazz with unique rhythms. Brazilians love sports, and their favorite sport is soccer, which they call *futebol*.

Brazilians eat a great deal of beef because cattle are raised in many areas of Brazil. A favorite dish in southern Brazil is **churrasco**, skewers full of grilled meats of all kinds. In America, restaurants serving Brazilian-style grilled meats called *churrascarias* have recently become quite popu-

lar. Other basic Brazilian ingredients include rice, black beans, and fresh fruits and vegetables. Brazil's national dish is **feijoada**, a stew of beef, pork, sausage, and black beans. The stew is simmered for a long time and served on special occasions with side dishes such as rice, orange slices, and shredded kale (a green leafy vegetable).

The Africans gave Brazilian food its spicy flavors and ingredients such as *malagueta* (a hot red pepper), coconut milk, and palm oil. Native Brazilians contributed many types of native fish and wild animals, sweet potatoes, corn porridge, hearts of palm, and manioc. **Hearts of palm** are the edible inner portion of the stem of the cabbage palm tree, which grows in many tropical climates and is Florida's official state tree. **Manioc**, also called cassava, is native to the Amazon rain forest. Once peeled, sweet manioc can be boiled and eaten like potatoes. It is also used to make flour.

The Portuguese heritage is seen in the Brazilian love for coffee and desserts that use a lot of eggs and sugar. For example, **quindim** is an upside-down dessert made with eggs, sugar, and grated coconut. The Portuguese also brought dried fruits to Brazil.

In the United States, Brazilian cooks might grill beef steaks, pork tenderloin, chicken, or a spicy sausage that is like Brazilian sausage. This recipe uses sirloin steak and includes a dipping sauce.

Time
40 minutes

Tools
measuring cups
measuring spoons
cutting board
paring knife
small bowl
whisk
broiling pan
oven mitts
spatula

Makes
4 servings

Ingredients

1 pound sirloin steak, 1 inch thick

1 teaspoon adobo seasoning

½ red onion

2 garlic cloves

⅛ cup red wine vinegar

¼ cup olive oil

1 teaspoon dried parsley

salt and pepper to taste

Steps

1. Season the steak with 1 teaspoon Adobo seasoning. Set aside.

2. Remove the papery skin from the red onion. Lay the onion half on its side on a cutting board. Slice and then chop into small pieces. Put ¼ cup chopped red onion in a small bowl.

3. Peel the papery skin from the garlic cloves. On a cutting board, mince. Add to the bowl with the red onion.

4. Add the red wine vinegar, olive oil, dried parsley, salt, and pepper to the onion and garlic. Whisk together well. Set aside as your sauce for the steak.

5. Preheat the broiler. Place the seasoned steak in the broiling pan. Using oven mitts, place the pan about 3 to 4 inches from the heat element or flame. Broil about 6 to 7 minutes, keeping an eye on the broiler at all times.

6. Using oven mitts, remove the pan from the oven. Turn the meat with a spatula and broil 6 to 7 minutes more for medium-doneness.

7. Using oven mitts, remove the pan from the oven. Turn the broiler off.

8. Slice the steak and serve immediately with the sauce on the side.

Classic Corn Cakes

Corn, which is a staple in Brazil, is used in many Brazilian American recipes, such as pudding and cookies. Enjoy these corn cakes with dinner.

Ingredients

vegetable oil cooking spray

1 tablespoon margarine

3 cups sugar

3 eggs

4 cups low-fat or nonfat milk

1½ cups yellow cornmeal

1½ tablespoons all-purpose flour

1 tablespoon baking soda

4 tablespoons Parmesan cheese

Steps

1. Preheat the oven to 350°F.

2. Spray a 9 × 13-inch baking pan with vegetable oil cooking spray.

3. Place the margarine in a small microwave-safe dish and put a lid on top. Heat on high power for about 20 seconds until melted.

4. In a large bowl, whisk the margarine, sugar, and eggs together.

5. Add the milk, and mix until well combined.

6. In a separate medium bowl, mix the cornmeal, flour, baking soda, and Parmesan cheese together with a wooden spoon.

7. Slowly add the dry ingredients to the milk mixture. Stir with a wooden spoon just until all of the dry particles are moistened.

8. Pour the batter into the baking pan. Use oven mitts to place pan in oven.

9. Bake at 350°F for about 30 to 35 minutes or until the top turns golden brown.

10. Use oven mitts to remove the pan from the oven. Allow to cool for at least 15 minutes before cutting into squares.

Time

15 minutes to prepare
plus
30 to 35 minutes to bake

Tools

measuring cups
measuring spoons
9 × 13-inch baking pan
small microwave-safe dish with lid
large bowl
whisk
medium bowl
wooden spoon
oven mitts

Makes

15 squares

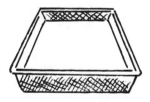

Fried Bananas with Cinnamon

Time
10 minutes

Tools
cutting board
paring knife
large frying pan
measuring spoons
spatula

Makes
2 to 4 servings

Brazilians cook fried bananas and serve them with meals or as dessert. Cinnamon trees grow in the tropical parts of Brazil.

Ingredients

2 ripe bananas

1 tablespoon vegetable oil or margarine

1 teaspoon cinnamon or 1 tablespoon cinnamon sugar

Steps

1. Peel the bananas. Using a cutting board, cut the bananas in half lengthwise.

2. Heat the frying pan over medium heat for 2 minutes. Add the oil or margarine and heat for a minute.

3. Add the banana halves. Fry them on one side until golden brown, then turn with a spatula.

4. Once the second side is golden brown, put the bananas on plates. Sprinkle with cinnamon or cinnamon-sugar. Serve immediately.

China is a vast Asian country that touches borders with many other countries, including Mongolia, Russia, North Korea, Vietnam, Laos, Myanmar, India, Bhutan, Nepal, and Pakistan. Eastern China has a long coastline along the Yellow Sea, East China Sea, and South China Sea. Due to its varied landforms, such as mountains and valleys, China's climate can be very different depending on where you are. In the south, the climate is more tropical, meaning that it is hot and rain falls frequently year-round. In central China, there are four seasons, and in northern China winters are long and cold.

China is home to one of the world's oldest civilizations. The first emperor of China united seven states in 221 B.C. to create the Chinese Empire. China was ruled by emperors until 1911. Today, China is run by a communist government.

Few Chinese came to America until after gold was discovered in California in 1848. Most of the early Chinese immigrants left from Guangdong Province in southern China. Although the Chinese were forbidden to leave their country, Guangdong was far away from the ruling forces in Beijing and had large, busy seaports. Famine and political unrest motivated Chinese laborers and merchants to travel to America in search of money. Most Chinese hoped to make enough money in America so that they could return to China and buy property, but many stayed.

Once in America, the Chinese mined for gold, farmed, and built railroads. The Chinese were recruited to build the transcontinental railroad, especially between Sacramento, California, and Promontory Point, Utah. This portion of the railroad was the hardest and most dangerous to build. It meant working in hot deserts, blasting rock with dynamite, and surviving harsh winters. Despite all their work to make the transcontinental railroad, which became a reality in 1869, the Chinese were referred to pejoratively as "coolies," an offensive term used to describe unskilled workers from China and other Asian countries.

Most Chinese immigrants settled together in neighborhoods that were eventually referred to as "Chinatowns," in cities such as San Francisco and New York. Americans had little knowledge of Chinese culture or customs. To the Americans, the Chinese immigrants looked different—they wore loose-fitting clothes and they pulled their hair back into pigtails. Americans often resented the Chinese not only for their customs but also because they were competing for jobs or gold.

In 1868, the United States and China signed a treaty that allowed Chinese people to come to the United States and guaranteed that the Chinese would not be discriminated against. Unfortunately, discrimination continued against the Chinese, and in 1882, Congress passed a law that forbade the immigration of Chinese laborers but allowed merchants, teachers, students, and tourists to immigrate. This law stayed in force until 1943, when any Chinese immigrant could enter the United States, but only 105 were allowed to enter each year.

In 1965, a new law greatly expanded the number of Chinese immigrants to 20,000 per year (this law is still in effect today). Chinese immigrated to the United States in great numbers to join their families, to study, and to work or practice their professions. Chinese Americans have come a long way since their customs and clothes were considered odd. They continue to work hard, as they did on the railroad, and many own businesses and work in professional fields.

Along with their love for the arts, such as poetry, and sports, such as Ping-Pong, the Chinese brought to America their cooking traditions. It is not unusual for the Chinese cook to shop once or twice a day for fresh ingredients. A meal includes foods with a balance of colors, flavors, and textures. For example, soft steamed vegetables may be served with crispy spring rolls.

Stir-frying is the most common way to cook Chinese food. Stir-frying involves cooking bite-sized pieces of food, such as cut-up chicken and vegetables, over medium-high heat in a small amount of oil while stirring constantly. Moving the foods around in the pan ensures that they cook evenly and quickly. Stir-frying rarely takes more than five minutes and is usually done in a **wok**, a large all-purpose Chinese pan.

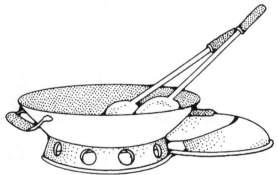

Rice and other grains, vegetables, and foods made from soybeans, such as soy sauce, bean sprouts, and tofu, are probably the most important Chinese ingredients. Plain rice is served at most meals. Sometimes fried rice is served. Fried rice is made by adding egg, vegetables, and sometimes meat to plain rice and stir-frying it. In northern China, noodles are often used in place of rice because the climate is not suitable for growing rice. Wheat is used to make dumplings, which are stuffed with ground meats and/or vegetables.

Some interesting fruits and vegetables used in Chinese cooking include the following:
- Chinese cabbage, also called **bok choy**
- Snow peas

- Water chestnuts
- **Kumquats** (a small fruit that resembles an orange but is not a citrus fruit)
- **Litchis** (a round, red fruit with a raisinlike flavor)

The Chinese use a wide variety of sauces, vinegars, herbs, and spices when cooking. Perhaps the most important ingredient is soy sauce, which is made from soybeans. **Hoisin sauce** is a dark, sweet sauce made from soybeans, sugar, and spices. **Oyster sauce** is a thick, brown sauce made from oyster extracts, sugar, and seasonings. With its sweet, smoky flavor, it really does not taste like oysters. Chinese hot mustard sauce is quite spicy, and is used as a dipping sauce for fresh vegetables, appetizers, cold meats, and egg rolls. **Plum sauce**, also called **duck sauce** because it is often served with roast duck, is made from plums, apricots, and other ingredients. It is also popular as a dipping sauce. Common spices are Sichuan pepper, star anise (which tastes like licorice), ginger, and sesame seeds.

A typical Chinese meal has no main dish. Instead, several dishes are served at once with rice, noodles, or pancakes. Examples of Chinese dishes include stir-fried chicken with snow peas; Sichuan shrimp; sweet and sour chicken with bell peppers, onions, and pineapple; and mu shu pork—stir-fried pork and vegetables wrapped in a Chinese pancake.

Soup may also be served. Wonton soup usually contains carrots, bok choy, and wontons. Wontons are round noodles filled with ground meats and vegetables. Egg drop soup, also called egg flower soup, is made with vegetables, possibly seaweed, and eggs, which are stirred in just before serving.

Tea, the main beverage, plays an important role in the life of the Chinese. People drink it anytime and anywhere. It is always drunk black—without cream, milk, sugar, or lemon.

Dessert is always fruit, except on special occasions. The fortune cookies served at many Chinese restaurants in the United States are not truly Chinese. Almond cookies, however, are an authentic Chinese sweet.

Lo mein *is a Chinese dish of boiled noodles combined with various stir-fried ingredients, such as chicken and vegetables. The cooked noodles are tossed with the stir-fried ingredients at the last minute to heat and coat all of the ingredients with the stir-fry sauce.*

Ingredients

1   package Chinese egg noodles

1   tablespoon dark sesame oil

8   bok choy leaves

2   boneless chicken breasts

¼   cup soy sauce

2   teaspoons cornstarch

1   teaspoon water

¼   cup low-sodium chicken broth

2   tablespoons oyster sauce

½   teaspoon sugar

3   tablespoons peanut oil

1   cup frozen sliced carrots, thawed

Steps

1. Bring a large pot of water to a boil. Carefully add the noodles to the boiling water, stirring with wooden spoon to separate. Cook for about 2 minutes, stirring several times, until they are firm but cooked through.

2. Using oven mitts, ask an adult to drain the noodles into a colander. Put the noodles back into the pot and toss with the sesame oil. Set aside.

3. Wash the bok choy and pat dry with paper towels. On a cutting board, slice the bok choy across the ribs into ¼-inch slices.

4. On a cutting board, cut the chicken into 1-inch pieces.

5. Mix the soy sauce, cornstarch, and water together in a medium bowl.

6. Add the chicken to the soy sauce mixture and coat well.

7. In a small bowl, whisk the chicken broth, oyster sauce, and sugar together. Set aside. You will use this toward the end of the stir-fry.

Time
30 to 40 minutes

Tools
large pot
oven mitts
colander
wooden spoon
measuring cups
measuring spoons
paper towels
cutting board
paring knife
medium bowl
small bowl
whisk
wok or heavy frying pan with lid
slotted spoon
large bowl

Makes
4 servings

8. Heat 1 tablespoon of peanut oil on medium-high heat in the wok or heavy frying pan. Add the bok choy and carrots. Cover and cook for about 3 minutes until the bok choy has wilted. Remove with a slotted spoon and place into a large serving bowl.

9. Heat another tablespoon of peanut oil on medium-high heat in the wok. Stir-fry the chicken pieces for about 5 minutes until cooked through. Remove from the wok. Add to the serving bowl and toss.

10. Heat the remaining 1 tablespoon of peanut oil on medium-high heat. Add the cooked noodles and stir-fry until they are heated.

11. Stir in the vegetables and chicken. Add the oyster sauce mixture, cover, and cook for 2 minutes.

12. Return to the serving bowl and serve.

Sichuan-Style Beef Stir-Fry with Rice

Each region of China has its own special dishes. Sichuan is the province in south-central China known for its spicy food. Sichuan cooks prefer strong flavorings, such as garlic and chiles, as well as hot spices such as Sichuan pepper. Sichuan peppercorns are the dried berries of a native plant.

Ingredients

¾ cup dry long-grain white rice

4 scallions

6 button mushrooms

1 red pepper

⅓ cup teriyaki sauce

½ cup beef broth

3 tablespoons Sichuan sauce

2 tablespoons cornstarch

1 pound skirt steak

½ teaspoon salt

¼ teaspoon pepper

2 tablespoons peanut oil

2 cups frozen broccoli florets, thawed

2 cups frozen snow peas, thawed

1 14-ounce can baby corn

Steps

1. Cook the rice in a medium saucepan according to package directions. Leave in covered saucepan to keep warm.

2. Wash the scallions, mushrooms, and red pepper. Pat dry with paper towels.

3. Using a cutting board, cut the roots off the scallions and cut the stems off the mushrooms. Cut the scallions and mushrooms into ¼-inch slices. Slice only the lower third of the scallions' green tops next to the white root end.

4. On a cutting board, cut the red pepper in half. Remove and discard the stem, seeds, and ribs. Cut the pepper into strips, then dice.

5. In a small bowl, whisk the teriyaki sauce, beef broth, Sichuan sauce, and cornstarch together.

6. Using a cutting board, slice the skirt steak diagonally into ¼-inch strips. Sprinkle with salt and pepper.

Time
40 minutes

Tools
measuring cups
measuring spoons
medium saucepan with lid
paper towels
cutting board
paring knife
small bowl
whisk
wok or heavy skillet
wooden spoon
can opener
slotted spoon
colander
large bowl

Makes
6 servings

7. In a wok or heavy frying pan, heat the peanut oil over medium-high heat for 2 minutes. Add the steak and use the wooden spoon to stir-fry for about 3 minutes or until browned. Remove the steak with a slotted spoon.

8. Add the scallions, mushrooms, and red pepper. Stir-fry for 2 to 3 minutes.

9. Open the can of baby corn and drain in a colander. Add the baby corn, broccoli, and snow peas to the wok. Continue to stir-fry for 2 to 3 minutes.

10. Place the steak back in the wok.

11. Stir the teriyaki sauce mixture into the wok. When the liquids thicken and the vegetables are coated with a thin glaze, turn off the wok.

12. Place the rice in a large bowl and pour the stir-fry over the rice. Serve.

Ginger-Scented Fruits with Orange Sorbet

The Chinese brought with them a love for exotic fruits, such as litchis and mandarin oranges, that grow in their country. Americans have taken some of these fruits and created new dishes like this one.

Ingredients

1 15-ounce can litchis

1 10-ounce can mandarin oranges

1 star fruit

1 kiwi

1 lime

1 pint orange sorbet

1 tablespoon chopped crystallized ginger

Steps

1. Drain the litchis and mandarin oranges and set aside.

2. Wash and pat dry the star fruit and lime with paper towels.

3. On a cutting board, slice the star fruit (the peel is edible).

4. Peel and slice the kiwi.

5. On a piece of waxed paper, use a grater or a zester to remove 1 teaspoon of zest from the lime. Zest is the colored, outermost layer of skin that has the flavor of the fruit. Do not remove the white part of the skin—it has a bitter taste.

6. Scoop the orange sorbet onto 4 dessert plates. Arrange the litchis, oranges, star fruit, and kiwi on each plate around the sorbet.

7. Sprinkle the lime zest and ginger on top of each plate as a garnish and serve immediately.

Time
15 minutes

Tools
measuring spoons
can opener
paper towels
cutting board
paring knife
vegetable peeler
waxed paper
zester or grater
scoop
4 dessert plates

Makes
4 servings

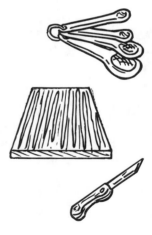

CHAPTER 3

CUBA

Cuba is the northernmost island in a chain of Caribbean islands that includes Puerto Rico, Jamaica, and Hispaniola. About the size of Ohio, it lies between the Caribbean Sea and the Atlantic Ocean. Florida is only 90 miles north. The Republic of Cuba, its official name, has many sandy beaches, as well as mountains and farmland. Due to the warm climate, many crops, such as bananas, grow well.

Before Europeans arrived, two groups of native Cubans lived on the island of Cuba and fished, farmed, and made pottery. When the Spanish arrived in Cuba in the early 1500s, the native Cuban population was wiped out as a result of disease and mistreatment. Cuba was a Spanish colony for many years, and Spanish is still its national language.

Over half a million Africans were brought to Cuba during the early and mid-1800s to work as slaves on the large sugar plantations. Sugarcane continues to be grown for export to other countries.

With the help of the U.S. Army, in 1898 the Cubans won their independence from Spain. The young republic had many problems, however, especially with poor leadership. In 1959, rebels led by a general named Fidel Castro used force to take over Cuba's government. In 1960, Castro strengthened Cuba's ties with the Soviet Union, and Cuba's government became communist (a system of government in which property is not owned by individuals but is shared by the community).

Most of the Cubans who came to America during the early 1960s came to escape the government, which took over the sugar plantations, ranches, private businesses, and properties of many scientists, doctors, teachers, artists, and writers. Some Cubans were able to come to America by plane, but many had to endure dangerous, overcrowded boat rides to freedom. Also, many Cubans left so hastily that they lacked the proper paperwork to remain in the United States, and those who did stay often had a hard time finding jobs using their skills. Many Cubans settled in Miami, which is 150 miles from Cuba. Miami became like a second Havana (the capital of Cuba).

Music and dancing are important in the Cuban culture. Cuban music has both African and Spanish roots. African drums, such as the conga and bongos, and the Spanish guitar are often heard in Cuban music. **Son** is the native dance music of Cuba and is over 200 years old. In son the rhythm is tapped out on two heavy wooden sticks called *claves*, while a singer sings and additional instruments play. *Salsa*, a popular music style in America, is based on son as well as other Latin American rhythms and jazz. The **rumba**, an Afro-Cuban dance style, is based on drum rhythms.

When Cubans came to America, they brought with them a rich cooking tradition. Cuban cooking is a mix of traditional Spanish foods (such as olives), African foods (such as plantains—large bananas that must be cooked), and vegetables that grow in the Caribbean climate. Also popular are fruits that grow well in warm climates, such as oranges, bananas, mangoes, and papayas. For side dishes and in stews, Cuban cooks use several unique starchy vegetables, including

- **Boniato**: A Cuban sweet potato with white or yellow flesh rather than orange flesh. It tastes a bit like chestnuts.
- **Yucca** (also known as cassava): Has a mild buttery flavor and is used like a potato. It is often boiled and served with garlic sauce.
- **Malanga**: Similar to a yam, it has an earthy flavor and is often made into chips and used in soups and stews.

Cuban dishes frequently contain tomatoes, garlic, peppers, onions, lime, and olives. These common ingredients are flavorful but not too spicy. Staple Cuban foods include rice and beans, especially black beans. Rice and beans are commonly served together, and rice is present at almost every meal. Cuban dishes include

- **Moros y cristianos**: This is Spanish for "Moors and Christians." The Moors were Muslim Arabs who occupied southern Spain centuries ago. They were driven out of Spain by Christians. The dish includes white rice, black beans, onions, garlic, green peppers, and tomatoes.
- **Arroz con pollo**: This is Spanish for "rice with chicken." It is flavored with tomatoes, olives, capers, peppers, and raisins.
- **Picadillo**: This dish with ground beef is flavored with olives, raisins, tomatoes, peppers, and onions. Picadillo is served with rice (raisins are usually mixed in) and sometimes has a fried egg on top.
- **Ropa vieja**: This is Spanish for "old clothes." The dish features spicy shredded strips of beef with vegetables.
- **Chicharrones de pollo**: Small pieces of chicken are marinated in lime juice and soy sauce; then they are breaded and fried.

To prepare some of these dishes, garlic, onion, and bell peppers are first sautéed in olive oil until soft and fragrant. This sauce is called *sofrito* and is the basis for many Cuban dishes. Sofrito and mojo have been adopted by a number of American cooks. **Mojo** is a sauce of garlic, citrus juice, oil, and fresh herbs that is added to food at the table.

For dessert, **flan** is popular. Flan is a baked custard with caramel topping. Another dessert is guava pastries. **Guava** is a pale green pear-shaped tropical fruit that is only 2 to 3 inches long. When ripe, the guava is sweet and moist. Guava can be eaten fresh or boiled, and it is used as a sweet pastry filling.

Cuban immigrants have made significant contributions to American food and cooking, both within and outside of Cuban communities. Today, Americans and Cubans alike enjoy foods such as Cuban sandwiches for lunch and arroz con pollo for dinner. Of course, some Cuban eating traditions have changed. For example, a traditional Cuban breakfast of toasted Cuban bread (like a sourdough bread) and café con leche (strong coffee with frothed milk) is often supplemented with eggs or other American breakfast foods. The Cuban sandwich has also been Americanized. The traditional sandwich includes roast pork, ham, cheese, and dill pickle on Cuban bread brushed with butter or olive oil. The sandwich is then flattened and browned. The newer version is mounded high on Cuban bread with lettuce, tomatoes, and mayonnaise instead of olive oil. Some American chefs are also spicing up Cuban food, using hotter peppers and more herbs and spices.

To make the traditional toasted and flattened Cuban sandwich, restaurants use a special press called a plan-cha. In this recipe you will use a heavy skillet to press down on the sandwich while you grill it. Cuban bread is best for this sandwich, although French bread will do. However, don't use a baguette, because it is too narrow to press correctly. Cuban bread is baked differently than French bread, making it lighter and crisper.

Ingredients

1 long loaf Cuban or French bread

4 tablespoons butter

½ pound Virginia ham, sliced

½ pound lean roasted pork, sliced

¼ pound Swiss cheese, sliced

16 dill pickle slices

vegetable oil cooking spray

Time
15 minutes

Tools
cutting board
knife
measuring spoons
spreader
nonstick skillet
heavy skillet (to press the sandwiches down)
spatula

Makes
4 sandwiches

Steps

1. Using a cutting board, cut the bread into 4 sections, each about 6 inches long. Cut each section of bread lengthwise.

2. Spread about 1 tablespoon of butter on the insides of each sandwich.

3. Layer ham, pork, cheese, and 4 pickle slices inside each sandwich.

4. Spray a nonstick skillet with vegetable oil cooking spray.

5. Preheat the skillet over medium heat for 2 minutes. Add the sandwiches. You may have to cook 2 sandwiches at a time.

6. Place a heavy iron skillet on top of the sandwiches to flatten. Try to flatten the sandwiches to about half their original size.

7. Grill the sandwiches for 2 to 3 minutes on each side, using the spatula to turn the sandwiches over, until the cheese is melted and the bread is golden.

8. Lift the sandwiches carefully out of the skillet and onto plates. Slice in half diagonally and serve.

Banana Strawberry Batidos

Time
10 minutes

Tools
cutting board
paring knife
blender
colander
paper towels
measuring cups
measuring spoons
2 tall glasses

Makes
2 servings

Batidos *are icy Cuban drinks that are as common as cola in cities with many Cuban residents, such as Miami. Batidos come in different flavors, such as banana strawberry or mango papaya. They're easy to make—just put your ingredients in the blender and whirl!*

Ingredients

2 small ripe bananas
1 cup strawberries
1 lime
1 tablespoon sugar

¾ cup low-fat or nonfat milk
2 tablespoons sweetened condensed milk
1½ cups crushed ice

Steps

1. Peel the bananas. Using a cutting board, cut the bananas into 1-inch slices. Put the banana slices into the blender.

2. Put the strawberries in a colander and wash under cold running water. Pat dry with paper towels.

3. On the cutting board, use the paring knife to cut the tops off the strawberries. Cut each berry into 4 pieces and add to the blender.

4. Slice the lime in half. Squeeze enough juice from the lime to make 1 tablespoon, and add this juice to the blender.

5. Put the sugar, milk, and condensed milk into the blender. Blend until the fruits are smooth.

6. Add the crushed ice and blend for 15 seconds.

7. Pour the batidos into tall glasses and serve immediately.

···· Cuban Black Bean ···· Soup

When the Cubans came to America, they brought this famous soup. It may be slightly different from the original, because Cuban Americans may use bacon or sausage instead of the traditional ham hocks in the soup, and they may substitute some seasonings.

Ingredients

1 small onion
1 green pepper
2 garlic cloves
1 stalk celery
4 bacon slices
1 tablespoon olive oil

1 teaspoon ground cumin
2 cups canned black beans, drained and rinsed
4 cups water
1 tablespoon red wine vinegar
¼ teaspoon salt

Steps

1. Remove the papery skin from the onion. On a cutting board, cut the onion in half. Place the flat side down and chop each onion half into small pieces.

2. Wash the pepper and pat dry with paper towels. Cut the pepper in half. Remove and discard the seeds and ribs. Cut the pepper into strips. Chop each strip.

3. Peel the papery skin from the garlic cloves. Chop the garlic.

4. Wash the stalk of celery and pat dry with paper towels. Cut the celery into ¼-inch slices.

5. Cut the bacon slices into small pieces.

6. Preheat a large pot or Dutch oven on medium-high heat for 2 to 3 minutes. Add the olive oil.

7. Add the chopped onion, green pepper, garlic, celery, and bacon and sauté for about 3 minutes. Stir in the cumin and cook 1 more minute.

8. Add the beans, water, vinegar, and salt to the pot. Bring to a simmer and cook for 30 minutes to develop flavors. Stir occasionally with wooden spoon.

9. Ladle into 4 soup bowls and serve immediately.

Time
1 hour

Tools
cutting board
paring knife
paper towels
large pot or Dutch oven
measuring cups
measuring spoons
can opener
wooden spoon
ladle
4 soup bowls

Makes
4 servings

CHAPTER 4

THIOPIA

Ethiopia is located on the eastern side of the African continent. It is surrounded by the countries of Eritrea, Dijbouti, Somalia, Kenya, and Sudan. Central Ethiopia is a plateau surrounded by lowlands. The climate on the plateau is balmy and pleasant, with rain in the summer months. The lowlands tend to be hotter and have less rain.

Except for when Italy briefly controlled Ethiopia from 1935 to 1941, Ethiopia has a long history of being an independent country and is somewhat isolated. Ethiopia's people are very diverse, with many native groups and over 50 languages spoken. Many of its people are Muslims or Christians.

In the past, war, diseases, drought, and famine have taken their toll on Ethiopia's people, causing some to immigrate to America and other countries. Most of the Ethiopians who came to America came after the

Immigration Act of 1965. After West Africa, Ethiopia is the second-largest source of African immigrants to the United States. Most Africans who have arrived here in the last 20 years have improved their quality of life through better jobs and education.

Ethiopia's culture has been influenced by its many ethnic groups and Christian and Muslim religions. Every ethnic group has its own songs that are passed down from generation to generation, ranging from household songs to hunting songs and religious songs. Dance is also important as a community activity, and almost every ethnic group has its own distinct dance.

Ethiopians who live in the United States have brought their love of foods with names such as injera and wat. **Injera** is the staple food of Ethiopia. It is a very flat, spongy bread, almost like a pancake, with a slightly bitter taste. Injera is made mainly with a flour made from teff, an Ethiopian grain that is tiny and round and flourishes in the highlands. Injera is prepared the same way today as it was 1,000 years ago. The batter is poured into a pan and baked until it looks like a thin rubber sponge. For meals, a large round injera is laid on the table and the hot foods are piled on it. Ethiopians wrap a piece of injera around the hot foods and tear it off to be eaten. In this manner, injera acts as both a plate and utensils.

Wat is a peppery stew made with meat and/or vegetables. The meat is usually lamb, beef, or chicken. Neither Muslims nor Ethiopian Christians eat pork. Wat may also include fish. Twice a week, Ethiopian Christians do not eat any meat, so they eat wat made only with vegetables such as chickpeas, lentils, and potatoes.

Ethiopians were the first to cultivate the coffee plant. Ethiopian coffee is rich and delicious. Sweetened tea is also on hand for those who don't like coffee.

···· Ethiopian Injera ····

Injera bread is made from three ingredients: teff flour, water, and salt. Teff is a very important grain grown in Ethiopia. You can use whole-wheat flour and biscuit mix to replace the teff flour. Injera is usually served with a stew on top. The injera is then wrapped around the stew and eaten.

Ingredients

1   cup whole-wheat flour
1   cup biscuit mix
1   egg

1 ½ cups water
vegetable oil cooking spray

Steps

1. In a medium bowl, combine the whole-wheat flour and biscuit mix. Mix together with a wooden spoon.

2. In a small bowl, beat the egg with a fork.

3. Add the egg and water to the flour mixture and stir until well combined.

4. Preheat the oven to 325°F.

5. Spray a large oven-safe frying pan with vegetable oil cooking spray. Preheat on medium-high heat for 2 minutes.

6. Pour about one-fifth of the batter onto the skillet in a thin stream starting from the outside of the pan and spiraling around to the center.

7. Cook the flat bread for about 2 minutes or until the surface is bubbly. Turn off the heat.

8. Using oven mitts, place the pan in the oven for 2 to 3 minutes until the top is dry but not brown.

Time
45 minutes

Tools
measuring cups
medium bowl
wooden spoon
small bowl
table fork
large oven-safe frying pan
oven mitts
spatula
plate

Makes
5 flat breads

9. Take the pan out of the oven with oven mitts. Use a spatula to move the flat bread onto a plate.

10. Repeat until the batter is used up.

11. Serve the flat bread with Ethiopian Vegetable Bowl on top.

Ethiopian Vegetable Bowl

Ethiopians enjoy vegetable alecha, a spicy vegetable stew, on days when they can't eat meat, as well as at other times.

Ingredients

1 onion
1 green pepper
1 red pepper
2 carrots
2 potatoes
1 small head cabbage
2 tablespoons olive oil

3 cups water
1 cup diced tomatoes
1 6-ounce can tomato sauce
1 teaspoon salt
½ teaspoon pepper
½ teaspoon ground ginger

Steps

1. Remove the papery skin from the onion. Using a cutting board, cut the onion in half. Lay each onion half flat on the cutting board and chop into small pieces.

2. Wash the peppers, carrots, and potatoes. Pat dry with paper towels.

3. Cut the peppers in half. Scoop out the seeds and cut the ribs out carefully with a knife. Discard the seeds and ribs.

4. Lay the peppers flat-side down on the cutting board and cut into strips. Cut the strips into ¼-inch pieces.

5. Peel the carrots. Slice them into ¼-inch rounds.

6. Peel the potatoes. Slice them into ½-inch slices. Cut each slice in half.

7. Cut the cabbage in half. Remove the core, and rinse the remaining halves under running water. Pat dry with paper towels.

8. Place the cabbage halves flat-side down. Cut into ½-inch strips.

Time
20 minutes to prepare
plus
60 minutes to cook

Tools
cutting board
paring knife
paper towels
vegetable peeler
large frying pan with lid
or Dutch oven
measuring cups
measuring spoons
wooden spoon
can opener
large serving bowl

Makes
4 to 6 servings

9. Preheat a large frying pan or Dutch oven over medium heat for 2 minutes. Add the olive oil.

10. Cook the onions, peppers, and carrots until tender, stirring occasionally with a wooden spoon.

11. Add the potatoes, water, diced tomatoes, tomato sauce, salt, pepper, and ground ginger to the pot. Cook for 10 more minutes.

12. Add the cabbage to the pot and cover. Turn the heat to low and simmer the vegetables for an additional 40 minutes until tender.

13. Place in large serving bowl. Serve with injera.

Germany is located in the center of Europe, with Denmark to the north; Poland, the Czech Republic, and Austria to the east; Switzerland to the south; and France, Luxembourg, Belgium, and the Netherlands to the west. As you travel from the north to the south of Germany, you slowly climb from the lowlands by the seas to hilly regions and finally to the tall Alps. The climate varies but generally includes cold, snowy winters and warm summers.

Germans were the first major group of immigrants to settle in America who did not speak English. Beginning in 1683, Protestant Germans, persecuted by the Catholic rulers of Germany's small city-states, came to America to seek religious freedom. Other Germans came to America to get away from the disease, destruction, and starvation caused by religious wars. Many Germans were attracted to the first German settlement, called Germantown, just outside of Philadelphia, but Germans also settled from New York to Virginia. At the time of the Revolutionary War, over 250,000 Germans were in America.

The largest wave of German immigrants came to the United States from the 1830s through 1890. By 1850, the population of Germany had grown so large that many families had only small farms or limited means to make a living, so they came to America in hopes of building a better life. Some Germans also came as political refugees when they tried to revolt against governments to make them more democratic. Some Germans arrived in America as farmers and unskilled laborers, but many were skilled workers and tradespeople such as carpenters, printers, and bakers. During this immigration wave, Germans continued to settle in the northeast but also headed west and settled in midwestern areas such as Wisconsin and Missouri. German immigrants tended to live in German settlements, called Little Germany, both in the country and in cities such as New York, Baltimore, Chicago, Cincinnati, Milwaukee, and St. Louis.

As Germany became a prosperous nation, immigration to the United States continued but at a decreasing level. From 1933 to 1945, many Germans, especially Jews, fled when Adolf Hitler took over Germany and World War II started. Over the years, German Americans have made many contributions to American agriculture, business, science, the arts, and more.

German immigrants brought their language and culture with them to the United States. Germans are known for belonging to clubs, and indeed many Germans started social clubs, athletic clubs, church charities, and business associations in the United States. Music has always been a central part of German life. Germany certainly has a rich heritage of musicians and composers such as Ludwig von Beethoven. Many German Americans formed choruses, bands, orchestras, and singing societies. Oompah bands, originally from a region in Germany called Bavaria, are known for their music with its distinctive oom-pah-pah beat. Oompah bands continue to be popular in America.

The Germans also brought their cooking traditions to America. Germany is best known for its sausages. Different kinds of meats are cut up and mixed with spices to make sausages. Each region of Germany has its own way of making them. For example, the frankfurter was originally a type of sausage made in Frankfurt, Germany.

The Germans are well known for their baking. Germans make over 200 varieties of bread, including rye and pumpernickel. These breads are made using different types of rye flour. The Germans are also master bakers of pastries, such as streudel, and tortes (rich cakes). Pastries and tortes are eaten for an afternoon snack with coffee; children have them with milk.

Some German dishes that have become American favorites include the following:

- Frankfurters: The true German frankfurters are made in the Frankfurt am Main region of Germany. They must be made of 100 percent pork without any added fat or chemicals. Frankfurters are then smoked using traditional methods and sold in attached pairs. American frankfurters (or wieners or hot dogs) are made with pork, beef, chicken, turkey, or even tofu, and chemical additives are often used.

- Sauerkraut (meaning "sour cabbage"): Sauerkraut is cabbage that has gone through a special process (called fermentation) that gives it a unique, somewhat sour, taste. Although many think sauerkraut was a German invention, the Chinese actually created it as a way to keep cabbage fresh. The Germans really enjoy sauerkraut, and most of their cabbage crop is devoted to making sauerkraut using a variety of recipes.

- Sauerbraten (meaning "sour meat"): **Sauerbraten** is a favorite type of beef roast that is served as a main dish. Before the roast is cooked, it is marinated for several days in a mixture of vinegar and flavorings. This marinade tenderizes the meat and gives it a sour flavor. Although German recipes call for raisins and jelly to make it less sour, Americans often use crushed gingersnap cookies to add sweetness.

- Black Forest Cherry Torte: A torte is a cake with a rich frosting. Black Forest Cherry Torte is a chocolate cake that is filled and topped with whipped cream and cherry preserves. The Black Forest is a part of Germany where there are many orchards full of cherries, apples, and plums.

Bratwurst with Sauerkraut

Bratwurst *is a German sausage made with pork, or pork and veal, and spices. Bratwurst is common in the United States, especially in Wisconsin, where many German immigrants settled in the 19th century.* Brat *means "fry," and* wurst *means "sausage." Authentic bratwurst is a fresh sausage that must be cooked thoroughly before eating. Precooked bratwurst does not look or taste like fresh bratwurst. If you prefer to grill or broil the bratwurst without boiling it first, allow 20 more minutes of cooking time.*

Ingredients

4   fresh bratwurst

2   tablespoons vegetable oil

½ pound sauerkraut

1   tablespoon brown sugar

4   french rolls

ketchup and mustard as desired

Steps

1. Fill a large saucepan two-thirds full with water. Bring to a boil over high heat. Add the bratwurst.

2. When the water boils again, reduce the heat to low. Cover the pan and simmer for 10 minutes.

3. Using tongs, remove the bratwurst from the water.

4. Put the oil in a medium frying pan and heat on medium for 1 minute.

5. Add the bratwurst and panfry for 5 minutes. With a wooden spoon, turn frequently so that they brown evenly.

6. Add the sauerkraut and brown sugar to the pan. Continue cooking the bratwurst with the sauerkraut for 5 more minutes.

7. Split the french rolls with a bread knife. Place one-quarter of the sauerkraut down the middle of each roll. Put a bratwurst in each roll. Add ketchup and mustard as desired, and serve.

Time
30 minutes

Tools
large saucepan with lid
tongs
medium frying pan
measuring spoons
wooden spoon
bread knife

Makes
4 servings

···· German Potato ···· Salad

Time
50 to 60 minutes

Tools
vegetable scrub brush
paring knife
vegetable peeler
cutting board
large saucepan
long fork
colander
large bowl
medium frying pan
tongs
paper towels
wooden spoon
measuring cups
measuring spoons

Makes
8 servings

German potato salad is made with oil or bacon fat, vinegar, and bacon instead of mayonnaise. It tastes better warm or at room temperature than cold. If the salad has been refrigerated, let it stand at room temperature for 30 minutes before serving for the best flavor.

Ingredients

6   medium potatoes
1   large onion
8   slices bacon
3   tablespoons all-purpose flour
1   tablespoon sugar
1   teaspoon salt
1   teaspoon white pepper
½   cup apple cider vinegar
1   cup water

Steps

1. Scrub the potatoes with a brush under running water. Remove the eyes and any decayed areas with a paring knife. Peel the potatoes with a vegetable peeler. On a cutting board, cut the potatoes into ¼-inch slices.

2. Put the potatoes in the saucepan and add enough water to cover.

3. Bring the water to a boil over high heat. Simmer the potatoes for 20 minutes or until they are just tender.

4. While the potatoes boil, remove the papery skin from the onion. Using a cutting board, cut the onion in half. Chop each onion half.

5. Use a fork to prick the potatoes to see if they are just tender. When ready, turn the heat off. Ask an adult to drain the potatoes using the colander, then transfer them to the large bowl.

6. Put the frying pan on medium heat. Lay the bacon strips side by side in the pan. Cook for about 10 minutes. Turn the bacon over every 2 to 3 minutes with tongs.

7. Remove the bacon from the pan and place on paper towels.

8. Using a wooden spoon for stirring, sauté the onions in the bacon drippings until golden brown and tender, about 5 minutes. Add the flour and cook for 1 minute while stirring constantly.

9. Add the sugar, salt, pepper, vinegar, and water. Bring to a boil, then reduce the heat and simmer until the mixture just starts to thicken. Pour over the cooked potatoes.

10. Break up the bacon into small pieces and add to the potato salad. Toss gently and serve.

···· Gingerbread People ····

Time
30 minutes
plus
1 hour in refrigerator

Tools
measuring cups
measuring spoons
large bowl
wooden spoon
plastic wrap
2 cookie sheets
rolling pin
4 to 6-inch people-
shaped cookie cutters (or
any large cookie cutters)
oven mitts
spatula
wire rack

Makes
18 large cookies

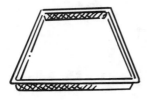

Germans brought their love for gingerbread cookies to America. The cookies are traditionally shaped into hearts, stars, people, and other forms. Large pieces of gingerbread are used to make gingerbread houses. The American version of gingerbread often uses fewer spices than the original German version.

Ingredients

¾ cup firmly packed brown sugar

½ cup softened butter (left at room temperature for 1 hour)

2 eggs

¼ cup molasses

3¼ cups all-purpose flour

2 teaspoons ground ginger

1½ teaspoons baking soda

½ teaspoon ground allspice

1 teaspoon ground cinnamon

1 teaspoon ground nutmeg

½ teaspoon salt

shortening

decorative candies (optional)

Steps

1. Put the brown sugar and butter in a large bowl. Press the butter and brown sugar against the bowl with the back of the wooden spoon until they are well mixed and creamy.

2. Add the eggs and molasses. Mix well.

3. Stir in the flour, ginger, baking soda, allspice, cinnamon, nutmeg, and salt. When mixed well, cover with plastic wrap and refrigerate the dough for 1 hour.

4. Preheat the oven to 350°F.

5. Use shortening to grease 2 cookie sheets.

6. Use a rolling pin to roll the dough out to ¼-inch thickness on a floured surface. Use 4- to 6-inch people-shaped cookie cutters dipped in flour to cut the dough. Place the cookies on the baking sheets, leaving 2 inches of space between cookies.

7. Use oven mitts to place cookies into oven. Bake the cookies for 8 to 10 minutes or until they start to brown.

8. With oven mitts, remove cookies from oven. Let the cookies cool for 1 minute, then use a spatula to transfer the cookies to a wire rack to continue cooling. If desired, decorate the cookies with candies.

CHAPTER 6

INDIA

Most of India, a country in southern Asia, is surrounded by water: the Arabian Sea to the west, the Indian Ocean to the south, and the Bay of Bengal to the east. India borders on Pakistan, China, Nepal, Bhutan, Bangladesh, and Myanmar.

The landscape and climate of India are quite diverse. The Himalayan Mountains to the north are quite cold, but southern India is warm year-round, if not downright hot. The Ganges Plain just south of the Himalayas is one of the most fertile areas in the world, and farmers there grow wheat, corn, barley, and other crops. Farther south where it is warmer, farmers grow rice, tropical fruits, vegetables, coffee, tea, and sugarcane.

Before 1965, only a few Indians came to America, mainly to get away from droughts, famine, conflicts, and hard times. Many of these early immigrants worked as laborers in logging, railroading, and farming on the west coast. After 1965, however, new immigration laws let more

••• 55

Indian immigrants enter the country. More of these immigrants were educated and skilled people looking for better opportunities. Today, Indian Americans live around the country, but larger numbers live on both the West and East Coasts, especially in New York and New Jersey.

Indian traditions of dance, art, literature, and music go back thousands of years. Music is very important in Indian culture. Singing is part of many religious rituals, such as saying prayers or a daily call to prayer, as well as at weddings, births, and harvest time, and even for welcoming a guest. Indian classical music uses a string instrument called a sitar, a pair of drums, and a wooden flute.

Food is also an important part of Indian culture. Indian food is known for being fragrant and sometimes spicy, because herbs and spices are such important ingredients. Various herbs and spices are mixed together to make a blend called **masala**. There are many types of masala, and each has its own unique flavor.

Religion influences what Indians eat. Most Indians are Hindu, and Hindu families will not eat beef because the cow is sacred in their religion. Many Hindus are vegetarian, so they do not eat any type of meat. Other Indians are Muslims, who practice Islam, which forbids the eating of pork.

Dishes from northern India include **tandoori**, a meat or chicken dish that is first marinated in lime juice, oil, and yogurt. Small chunks of the meat or poultry are then put on skewers and roasted in a clay oven called a *tandoor*.

Indians also enjoy curries and dals. **Curries** are spicy stews. When the British controlled India, they named any type of spicy stew a curry. When the British returned to England, they yearned for the taste of those spicy dishes, so a spice blend called curry powder was created. But really there are many different types of curry. Besides spices, curries may include chicken or lamb, cheese, nuts, and vegetables. **Dal** is a creamy vegetable dish made of legumes with vegetables, garlic, and spices. Legumes are a food group that includes dried lentils, beans, and peas. Lentils are the most commonly eaten legume in India.

Most Indian main dishes are accompanied by chutneys, raitas, or pickles. **Chutney** is a relish made from fruits and/or vegetables, and herbs and spices. It may taste sweet, sour, sweet and sour, salty, or hot. **Raita** is grated vegetables mixed with yogurt, like a salad. Chutney may be cooked, but raita is not. All kinds of fruits and vegetables are pickled, including lemons, limes, mangoes, and tomatoes. Indian pickles are known for their strong flavors.

Bread, such as a flat bread called **parantha**, is used to scoop up the food from plates. Besides parantha, Indians enjoy *chapati*, a round, flat bread made of wheat flour, and *naan*, a bread that uses yeast to make it rise (although it only rises a little). Fruit is often served as dessert and as a break from spicy foods. Favorite fruits include watermelon, papaya, pineapple, and mango. Indians also brought a love for sweets to America, such as **kulfi**, an Indian version of ice cream flavored with pistachio, mango, or other flavors.

Time

30 minutes to prepare
plus
2 hours to rise
plus
10 minutes to bake

Tools

measuring cups
measuring spoons
sifter
large bowl
small microwave-safe dish
with lid
medium bowl
table fork
whisk
wooden spoon
kitchen towel
cookie sheet or pizza
stone
pastry brush
oven mitts

Makes

8 servings

This traditional bread is made with yogurt, a staple of Indian cooking, and cooked in a tandoori oven. If you use a pizza stone to bake the bread in this recipe, it will come out crustier and more authentic.

Ingredients

3   cups all-purpose flour
1   cup whole-wheat flour
1   teaspoon baking powder
½   teaspoon baking soda
¼   teaspoon salt
2   tablespoons margarine

1   egg
1   cup low-fat or nonfat milk
¾   cup plain yogurt
    vegetable oil cooking spray
2   tablespoons margarine
1   tablespoon poppy seeds

Steps

1. Using a sifter, sift the flours, baking powder, baking soda, and salt together in a large bowl.

2. Place 2 tablespoons margarine in a small microwave-safe dish and put a lid on top. Microwave on full power for about 30 seconds or until melted.

3. Break the egg into a medium bowl. Beat with a fork.

4. Add the milk, yogurt, and melted margarine to the egg. Use a whisk to beat.

5. Make a shallow hole in the middle of the flour mixture. Pour the egg mixture into the well, and stir with a wooden spoon to form a soft dough.

6. Cover the dough with a kitchen towel and put in a warm place for 2 hours.

7. Preheat the oven to 400°F.

8. On a lightly floured surface, knead the dough for 2 to 3 minutes by pushing the dough away from you and then folding it over until the dough is smooth and silky.

9. Divide the dough into 8 pieces. Roll each piece of dough into a ball, then shape into a flattened oval about 6 inches long.

10. Spray a cookie sheet (or pizza stone) with vegetable oil cooking spray. Place the bread loaves on the cookie sheet (or pizza stone).

11. Again, place 2 tablespoons margarine in a small microwave-safe dish and put a lid on top. Microwave on full power for about 30 seconds or until melted.

12. Using a pastry brush, brush the bread loaves with the melted margarine. Sprinkle with poppy seeds.

13. Use oven mitts to put cookie sheet (or pizza stone) in oven. Bake at 400°F for 6 to 10 minutes until puffy and golden brown. Use oven mitts to remove the cookie sheet (or pizza stone) from the oven.

14. Let the bread sit for 10 minutes. Serve warm.

Curried Chicken

Time

30 minutes to prepare
plus
60 minutes to cook

Tools

measuring cups
measuring spoons
paper towels
cutting board
paring knife
vegetable peeler
large frying pan with lid
or Dutch oven
wooden spoon
can opener

Makes

4 servings

Indian cooking is known for its exotic spices. This recipe uses the spice blend known as curry powder that was developed outside of India to re-create the flavors of Indian foods for the British after they left India.

Ingredients

8   chicken thighs
½   teaspoon salt
¼   teaspoon pepper
2   celery ribs
1   Granny Smith apple
1   medium onion
1   garlic clove

2   tablespoons olive oil
1   14½-ounce can diced tomatoes
1   tablespoon curry powder
½   teaspoon cinnamon
1   tablespoon all-purpose flour
1   cup low-sodium chicken broth

Steps

1. Sprinkle the chicken thighs with salt and pepper.

2. Wash the celery and apple and pat dry with paper towels.

3. On a cutting board, slice the celery lengthwise into 2 pieces. Slice into ¼-inch slices.

4. Remove the papery skin from the onion. Cut the onion in half. With the flat sides down, cut the onion into small pieces.

5. Peel the apple. Cut the apple in half. Remove the core. Then lay flat and slice into ¼-inch slices.

6. Peel the papery skin off the garlic clove. Slice the garlic with a paring knife.

7. Preheat a large frying pan or Dutch oven on medium heat for 2 minutes. Add 1 tablespoon of the olive oil. Add the chicken and cook for 6 minutes on each side until golden brown. Remove the chicken from the pot.

8. Add the remaining 1 tablespoon of olive oil to the frying pan. Once hot, add the celery, onion, apple, and garlic. Stir with a wooden spoon for 2 to 3 minutes until tender.

9. Return the chicken to the frying pan. Add the diced tomatoes, curry powder, cinnamon, flour, and chicken broth. Stir together.

10. Cover and simmer on low for 1 hour. Serve immediately.

····· Basmati Rice ·····

Time
40 minutes

Tools
paper towels
cutting board
paring knife
measuring cups
measuring spoons
colander
large frying pan with lid
wooden spoon
serving bowl

Makes
6 servings

Basmati rice is grown in India. It has a special fragrance and nutty flavor and can be found in many American supermarkets. In this recipe, basmati rice is cooked with vegetables, raisins, and curry powder to make a delicious dish that can be served on the side or as a main course.

Ingredients

3 scallions	1 tablespoon curry powder
1 carrot	½ teaspoon salt
1 red bell pepper	¼ teaspoon pepper
1 cup basmati rice	½ cup raisins
2 tablespoons olive oil	½ cup sliced black olives
1½ cups vegetable broth	1 tablespoon dried parsley

Steps

1. Wash and pat dry the scallions, carrot, and red bell pepper.

2. On a cutting board, cut off the roots of the scallions. Slice the scallions into ¼-inch pieces, including 1 inch of the green stems next to the root end.

3. Slice the carrots into ¼-inch slices.

4. Cut the pepper in half. Scoop out the seeds, cut out the ribs, and discard. Cut the pepper into strips and dice.

5. Rinse the basmati rice in a colander several times. Set aside.

6. Preheat a large frying pan on medium heat for 2 minutes. Add the olive oil. Once hot, add the scallions and cook for 3 minutes until tender.

7. Add the basmati rice to the pan and stir until the rice is well coated with oil.

8. Add the vegetable broth and curry powder. Bring to a boil.

9. Stir in the salt and pepper.

10. Turn the heat to low. Cover and simmer for 15 minutes or until the rice is cooked and the broth is absorbed. Turn off the heat.

11. Add the carrots, red pepper, raisins, and olives to the basmati rice. Stir and cover, letting the rice rest for 10 minutes. Sprinkle with parsley.

12. Place in a serving bowl and serve.

CHAPTER 7

IRELAND

Ireland is an island, about the size of Maine, that is split into the Republic of Ireland and Northern Ireland, a province of the United Kingdom. Ireland has been called the "Emerald Isle" because of all the shades of green found in its landscapes. The abundant rainfall and mild temperatures encourage the growth of many kinds of plants.

The Irish have a long history of coming to America. Before America declared its independence from Great Britain in 1776, many of the Irish who came to this country were prompted by crop failures, high rents on their farmlands, and poor economic conditions. Beginning in the 1720s, many Irish came to America as indentured servants. In return for free passage, the indentured servants agreed to work for a wealthy landowner or merchant for three to four years, during which they received food and lodging but usually no wages. Many of these early immigrants settled in

Pennsylvania, attracted by the colony's religious tolerance and opportunities to earn a living.

The largest numbers of Irish came to America during the 1800s. The island of Ireland was ruled for many, many years by Great Britain. By 1700, the British, who were mostly Protestant, had taken away many rights from the Irish, who were mostly Catholic. The Irish Catholics also lost much of their land and wealth. Many had to live as peasants, renting small pieces of land on which to grow crops.

By the 1800s, the poor made up close to half of Ireland's population. Their daily diet consisted mostly of potatoes, which were eaten three times a day with milk or tea. Sometimes there was also some salted herring or fresh cabbage to eat. The peasants had not always eaten so poorly. Peasant farmers grew crops such as corn and wheat, but these were sold to pay the rent. Farmers were also given a small piece of land to grow their own food. Because potatoes were cheap and easy and fast to grow, farmers grew them for their families.

In 1845, a disease called potato blight ruined the potato crop for six long years. This period is called the Great Hunger. Many Irish died of starvation during this time, yet landowners continued to ship tons of wheat, corn, and other products to Britain. Record numbers of Irish left their country to go to America and other countries in search of jobs and food. Many Irish settled in northeastern cities such as Boston, New York, Philadelphia, and Baltimore. Others moved west to settle along the frontier, or simply moved to where there were jobs, for example, building canals and railroads.

The Irish brought with them a culture that is especially rich in literature and music. They love to tell stories in poetry and in a type of song called a ballad. Many Irish ballads talk about how the Irish felt over the centuries when they were ruled by others and parts of their culture were almost destroyed. For example, their language, called Gaelic, was outlawed by the English.

Many of Ireland's dishes, such as potato soup and Irish stew, were born during poor times. Irish stew shows how Irish cooks used potatoes, vegetables, and small amounts of meat to make dinner for an entire family. Originally made with goat meat, Irish stew was later made with lamb.

Potatoes are still the most commonly eaten vegetable, and Irish cooking serves up potatoes in many ways.

- **Dublin coddle**: A stew of potatoes, bacon, and ham.
- **Potato and leek soup**: A soup that includes leeks—a green and white vegetable with a mild onion flavor.
- **Boxty**: A type of potato bread that is baked or fried on a griddle like pancakes.

Other Irish American dishes are **Irish soda bread** and **Irish stew**. During the baking of Irish soda bread, a chemical reaction between the baking soda and the buttermilk or sour milk causes the bread to rise.

When the Irish came to America, they found some foods that were more plentiful and cheaper than in Ireland, so their recipes changed somewhat. For example, instead of making boiled bacon and cabbage as they had at home on the Irish holiday called Saint Patrick's Day, the Irish made corned beef and cabbage because beef and salt were cheaper than bacon. Corned beef was made by rubbing it with coarse "corns" of salt. *Corn* is an Old English word for a grain of salt. Salt was used long ago to keep meat from spoiling without refrigerators. Nowadays salt is used to give the beef a unique flavor.

Mom's Irish Soda Bread

Time
20 minutes to prepare
plus
50 to 60 minutes to bake

Tools
8 × 5-inch loaf pan
sifter
measuring cups
measuring spoons
large mixing bowl
wooden spoon
medium bowl
whisk
small microwave-safe dish with lid
rubber spatula
oven mitts

Makes
1 loaf (6 servings)

The original recipe for Irish soda bread included four ingredients: flour, baking soda, salt, and buttermilk or sour milk. Some ingredients have since been added to give the bread more flavor, such as sugar and raisins.

Ingredients

vegetable oil cooking spray
3 cups all-purpose flour
1 tablespoon baking powder
1 teaspoon baking soda
1 teaspoon salt

2 eggs
⅔ cup sugar
2 tablespoons shortening
2 cups buttermilk
1½ cups raisins

Steps

1. Preheat the oven to 350°F.

2. Spray an 8 × 5-inch loaf pan with vegetable oil cooking spray.

3. Using a sifter, sift the flour into a large mixing bowl.

4. Add the baking powder, baking soda, and salt to the bowl. Mix together with a wooden spoon.

5. In a medium bowl, beat the eggs with a whisk. Add the sugar and whisk together for about 3 minutes until creamy.

6. Place the shortening in a small microwave-safe dish with a lid. Microwave the shortening on full power for about 30 seconds or until liquid.

7. Add the shortening and buttermilk to the eggs and sugar. Whisk again until mixed.

8. Add the egg mixture to the flour mixture in the large mixing bowl. Stir with a wooden spoon just until all of the dry particles are moistened.

9. Fold in the raisins with a rubber spatula.

10. Put the dough in the loaf pan and use oven mitts to place in oven. Bake for approximately 50 to 60 minutes until the bread is lightly golden on top. Use oven mitts to remove the bread from the oven.

11. Let the bread sit for 10 minutes. Remove the bread from the pan. Cool completely before slicing.

Corned Beef and Cabbage Dinner

Time
About 3½ hours

Tools
paper towels
Dutch oven
meat fork
measuring cups
measuring spoons
2 plates
roasting pan
small mixing bowl
whisk
spreader
aluminum foil
paring knife
cutting board
large pot
table fork
oven mitts
knife for slicing meat
serving plate
colander
large serving bowl
serving spoon

Makes
8 servings

In many Irish American households in the United States, Saint Patrick's Day is celebrated on March 17 with a family gathering and a corned beef and cabbage dinner. Saint Patrick's Day is observed by the Catholic Church in honor of Saint Patrick, Ireland's patron saint, and is celebrated on the day of his death.

Ingredients

2 to 3 pounds lean corned beef
vegetable oil cooking spray
½ cup seedless raspberry jam
3 tablespoons creamy mustard
1 small head cabbage

2 pounds small, red new potatoes
1 teaspoon salt
½ teaspoon pepper
horseradish, mustard
¼ cup margarine

Steps

1. Wash the corned beef with water and pat dry with paper towels. Place into a Dutch oven and fill two-thirds full with water.

2. Place the Dutch oven on the stove on medium-high heat and bring the water to a boil.

3. Turn the heat down to low and cover. Simmer the corned beef for 2 hours.

4. With adult help, use a meat fork to remove the corned beef from the Dutch oven and place on a plate.

5. Measure out 1 cup of the liquid in which the corned beef was cooking. Set aside.

6. Preheat the oven to 325°F.

7. Spray a roasting pan with vegetable oil cooking spray and place the corned beef in the pan.

8. In a small mixing bowl, whisk the raspberry jam and the mustard together. Spread over the top of the corned beef. Cover loosely with aluminum foil.

9. Bake the corned beef in the oven for 45 to 60 minutes or until tender.

10. Meanwhile, wash the cabbage and pat dry. Cut the cabbage in half on a cutting board. With the flat sides down, slice the cabbage, shredding it into 1-inch strips.

11. Scrub the potatoes and pat dry. Cut the potatoes into quarters.

12. Place the cabbage, potatoes, salt, pepper, and saved liquid into a large pot. Place the pot on the stove on medium heat. When the liquid starts to boil, turn the heat to low and simmer for 45 minutes or until the potatoes are tender when poked with a fork.

13. When the corned beef is tender, use oven mitts to remove it from the oven. Let it rest for 15 minutes before slicing. Slice crosswise into 1/8-inch slices. Place on a serving plate. Serve with horseradish and/or mustard.

14. When the vegetables are tender, drain them into a colander (with adult supervision). Place the vegetables into a large serving bowl and add the margarine. Stir with a serving spoon and serve with the corned beef.

···· Anytime Apple and ···· Blackberry Pie

Time
35 minutes to prepare
plus
50 minutes to bake

Tools
measuring cups
measuring spoons
2 medium bowls
wooden spoon
pastry blender
table fork
2 plastic bags
paper towels
vegetable peeler
cutting board
paring knife
colander
rolling pin
9-inch pie pan
pastry brush
oven mitts
wire rack

Makes
1 9-inch pie (8 servings)

Apples and blackberries are two of Ireland's most adored fruits, and this pie is an Irish tradition. Instead of making your own piecrust, you can use two 9-inch circles of ready-to-bake pie dough.

Ingredients

Piecrust
2 cups all-purpose flour
1 teaspoon sugar
½ teaspoon salt
1¼ cups margarine
3–4 tablespoons cold water

Filling
6 Granny Smith apples
2 tablespoons lemon juice
1½ cups frozen blackberries
⅓ cup sugar
2 tablespoons all-purpose flour
½ teaspoon nutmeg
2 tablespoons low-fat or nonfat milk
1 tablespoon sugar

Steps

1. If you're using premade crust, skip to step 6. To make the piecrust, stir together the flour, sugar, and salt in a medium bowl with a wooden spoon.

2. Cut the margarine into the flour mixture with the pastry blender, using a back and forth motion until the mixture looks like small peas.

3. Sprinkle 1 tablespoon of the water over part of the mixture. Gently toss with a fork. Add 1 more tablespoon of water and toss again. Repeat 1 more time.

4. Use your hands to form the dough into a ball. If it is slightly dry, add ½ tablespoon of water. Repeat if necessary.

5. Divide the dough into 2 pieces and flatten each piece into a round disk. Place each disk into a plastic bag and place in the refrigerator to rest for 10 minutes.

6. Meanwhile, wash the apples and dry with paper towels. Peel the apples using a vegetable peeler.

7. On a cutting board, slice the apples in half with a paring knife. Cut out the core. With the flat sides down, slice each apple half into ¼-inch slices.

8. Place the apples in a medium mixing bowl filled with cold water and the lemon juice.

9. Drain the apples using a colander, and place them back into the mixing bowl. Add the frozen blackberries, sugar, flour, and nutmeg. Stir carefully with a wooden spoon.

10. On a lightly floured surface, use a rolling pin to roll 1 piece of dough into a 12-inch circle. Always roll from the center to the edges.

11. Roll the dough onto the rolling pin, then unroll the dough over a 9-inch pie pan. Use your hands to press the dough in place. Trim the pastry so that it is about ½ inch longer than the pie pan edges.

12. Preheat the oven to 375°F.

13. Place the apple filling into the pie pan.

14. Roll the second disk of dough into a 12-inch disk. Roll it onto the rolling pin, then unroll it over the pie filling. Trim the top crust so that it is about ½ inch longer than the pie plate and is even with the bottom crust.

15. To make a fluted edge around the pie, place your thumb against the inside of the pie crust. Press the dough around your thumb with your other hand's thumb and index finger.

16. Cut three small slices into the top of the pie so that heat can vent out.

17. Brush the milk on top of the pie with a pastry brush. Sprinkle the crust with sugar.

18. Use oven mitts to place pie in oven. Bake the pie for about 50 minutes or until the crust is golden brown. Take out of the oven with oven mitts and cool on a wire rack for 30 minutes before cutting.

CHAPTER 8

ITALY

Italy is located on a peninsula of Europe that juts out into the Mediterranean Sea. Two large islands, Sicily and Sardinia, are part of Italy, as well as smaller islands. Italy borders France, Switzerland, Austria, and Slovenia.

Italy has a lot of mountains and hills. The Alps curve across northern Italy, and another mountain range runs down the center of the country. Pastures for cattle, sheep, and goats are found in parts of the mountains. Farming is limited to some flat coastal areas, valleys, and the sloping sides of some foothills and mountains. Northern Italy has cold winters and hot, humid summers. Central and southern Italy have hot, dry summers and mild winters.

Unlike other Europeans, such as the Germans, who came to America during colonial times, most Italians came to America much later. The peak years of Italian immigration were from 1880 to 1914, when over 4 million Italians arrived. Most of the immigrants left Italy because of diseases, such as cholera, or crop failures and other economic hardships. Many Italian immigrants had been farmers, but few wanted that harsh existence in America. Newcomers often settled and took jobs in cities in New York, New Jersey, and Pennsylvania. Many cities on the East Coast had a Little Italy, a section where Italians lived together, often in cramped apartments in buildings called tenements. Although there were many Italians on the East Coast, many traveled west, and eventually Italians settled all across the United States.

As with other countries, Italy's foods vary from region to region because of different climates and landscapes. For example, cattle and dairy cows graze throughout northern Italy, so northern Italians eat much more beef and butter than people in other parts of the country. In southern Italy, where wheat is harvested and olive trees grow well in the warmer climate, people eat lots of pasta and olive oil. Olive oil is used in cooking and to dress salads. It is pale green and has a fruity, distinctive flavor.

Italians have created more than a hundred different pasta shapes. In northern Italy, where much corn and rice are grown, **polenta** (cornmeal porridge) and **risotto** (a creamy rice dish served with grated cheese) share the spotlight with pasta.

Seafood is particularly popular along Italy's extensive coastline, where there are many different species of fish and shellfish. Sausage is also very popular, and there are many varieties in Italy, including pepperoni and salami.

Italian cooking uses a wide variety of vegetables including onions, garlic, tomatoes, artichokes, eggplant, peppers, and zucchini. Favorite herbs include oregano, basil, and parsley.

Dairy cows produce milk that is used to make Italian cheeses such as mozzarella, ricotta, and Parmesan. Mozzarella cheese is best known as pizza cheese, and ricotta cheese is used in baked dishes such as lasagna and ziti. Parmesan cheese is a hard cheese that is grated and used in many Italian dishes.

The Italians brought their own types of appetizers, called **antipasto**, to America. The antipasto is something small, such as a wedge of cheese and some bread or marinated zucchini. Soups, salads, and pastas may also be served before the main entrée. Italian dressing is a simple dressing of olive oil, vinegar, and seasonings. Popular soups include minestrone (a hearty vegetable soup), pasta fagioli (a bean soup with pasta), and Italian wedding soup (with meatballs and spinach). The main course could be chicken, meat, or fish served with vegetables.

Dessert may be fruit or pastries such as cannolis or biscotti. Southern Italians brought their love for **cannoli**, a cream-filled pastry. **Biscotti**, meaning "cooked twice," are popular cookies. Biscotti are often served with gelato (ice cream) or fresh fruit. Ice cream is also a popular dessert. Italian ice cream is less creamy than American ice cream, and the flavors, such as strawberry, are much stronger. **Cappuccino**, a beverage made with espresso coffee and hot milk, is often served with dessert in America, but it is known as a breakfast beverage in Italy.

As Americans caught on to eating and making Italian foods, these foods often became less Italian and more American. For example, Italian pizza (which originated in Naples) is lighter than American pizza and contains less cheese and other toppings. Italian pizza crusts are always crispy.

Everyday Escarole, Bean, and Barley Soup

Time
30 minutes to prepare
plus
30 minutes to cook

Tools
paring knife
cutting board
paper towels
can opener
measuring cups
measuring spoons
colander
large pot or Dutch oven
wooden spoon
ladle
4 soup bowls

Makes
4 servings

Italians are known for their large meals, but at home a hearty soup, called zuppa *in Italian, accompanied by a loaf of Italian bread, is often the entire supper meal.*

Ingredients

1   medium onion
1   small bunch escarole
1   cup canned cannellini beans
½ cup chickpeas
2   tablespoons olive oil

1   teaspoon dried rosemary
1   teaspoon salt
¼ teaspoon pepper
½ cup pearl barley
5   cups low-sodium beef broth

Steps

1. Remove the papery skin from the onion. On a cutting board, cut the onion in half. Place the flat sides down and chop each onion half into small pieces.

2. Wash the escarole and pat dry with paper towels. Cut the escarole leaves into 1-inch pieces, discarding the stems. You should have about 5 cups of escarole leaves.

3. Drain the cannellini beans and chickpeas into a colander. Rinse and drain well.

4. Preheat a large pot or Dutch oven on the stove on medium heat for 2 minutes. Add the olive oil. Sauté the onions for 2 minutes until translucent.

5. Add the escarole, rosemary, salt, and pepper to the pot. Cook, stirring with a wooden spoon for about 5 minutes until the escarole is wilted.

6. Add the cannellini beans, chickpeas, and barley. Stir for 2 minutes.

7. Add the beef broth and simmer for about 30 minutes.

8. Use a ladle to serve in 4 soup bowls.

Savory Shrimp Dinner over Rice

From northern Italy to the Italian American tables of America, this recipe has been passed down through generations. Serve with a salad to complete the meal.

Ingredients

1 cup dry rice

2 lemons

1½ pounds extra large shrimp, peeled, cleaned, and deveined

4 tablespoons olive oil

2 teaspoons dried rosemary

1 teaspoon salt

¼ teaspoon pepper

1 teaspoon dried rosemary (for garnish)

Steps

1. Cook rice according to package instructions.

2. Preheat the broiler.

3. Roll the lemons on a flat surface to loosen the membranes. On a cutting board, cut the lemons in half.

4. Squeeze each lemon half over a measuring cup to collect the juice. Remove pits. Measure ⅓ cup of the lemon juice and set aside.

5. Place the shrimp in a medium mixing bowl. Toss the lemon juice, olive oil, 2 teaspoons of rosemary, salt, and pepper with the shrimp. Mix with a wooden spoon until well coated.

6. Place the shrimp in an oven-proof shallow baking dish. Using oven mitts, place the shrimp under the broiler for 5 minutes. Keep an eye on the shrimp as they cook.

7. Using oven mitts, take the shrimp out of the oven, and turn them over with a fork. Place under the broiler again, and broil 2 to 4 minutes more.

8. Sprinkle 1 teaspoon of rosemary on top of the shrimp. Serve shrimp over rice.

Time
20 to 25 minutes

Tools
measuring cups
measuring spoons
cutting board
paring knife
medium mixing bowl
wooden spoon
shallow broiler-proof baking dish
oven mitts
table fork

Makes
4 servings

Filomena's Love Knot Cookies

This recipe is a for a traditional Italian holiday cookie.

Time
60 minutes

Tools
2 cookie sheets
2 small bowls
measuring cups
measuring spoons
whisk
2 medium bowls
hand-held electric mixer
wooden spoon
oven mitts
wire rack
spatula
teaspoon

Makes
4 to 5 dozen cookies

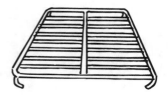

Ingredients

vegetable oil cooking spray
5 eggs
1 cup softened butter (left at room temperature for 1 hour)
1 cup softened cream cheese (left at room temperature for 1 hour)
1 cup sugar
3 tablespoons vanilla extract

5 cups all-purpose flour
5 tablespoons baking powder
¼ teaspoon salt

Icing
½ cup confectioner's sugar
1 tablespoon lemon extract
2 tablespoons water
sprinkles

Steps

1. Preheat the oven to 400°F. Spray 2 cookie sheets with vegetable oil cooking spray.

2. Break the eggs into a small bowl and whisk until smooth.

3. In a medium bowl, use a hand-held mixer on medium speed to cream the butter and cream cheese until smooth (about 3 minutes).

4. Add the sugar, eggs, and vanilla extract. Continue to beat until smooth and creamy.

5. In another medium bowl, whisk the flour, baking powder, and salt together.

6. Blend the flour mixture into the egg mixture with a wooden spoon until it resembles a soft dough. Be careful not to overmix.

7. Roll the dough into balls, using about 1 tablespoon of dough for each cookie. Place on cookie sheets about 2 inches apart.

8. Use oven mitts to place cookies in oven. Bake the cookies for 10 to 12 minutes until done. Do not brown.

9. Meanwhile, in another small bowl, whisk the confectioner's sugar, lemon extract, and water together. This will be the icing.

10. Take the cookies out of the oven with oven mitts.

11. Let cool 1 minute, then transfer to a wire rack with a spatula.

12. Drizzle the icing over the cookies with a teaspoon and drop sprinkles on them.

CHAPTER 9

LEBANON

Lebanon is a tiny country located on the Mediterranean Sea in the heart of the Middle East. Syria borders Lebanon to the north and east, and Israel borders southern Lebanon. Most food is grown in a fertile valley in the middle of Lebanon between two mountain ranges. Lebanese crops, such as citrus fruits and wheat, get plenty of sun and warmth, and rain is abundant, especially in winter.

Lebanon has a long history of being invaded and controlled by outsiders, including people from Egypt, Turkey, and France. In 1943, Lebanon became an independent Arab country. Many Lebanese are Muslims; however, unlike other Arab countries, Lebanon is also home to a large Christian population. Due mostly to friction between the Muslims and the Christians, Lebanon experienced a long civil war from 1975 to the early 1990s. The constant fighting and economic problems at that time caused many Lebanese to come to the United States (as well as other countries) for better educational and economic opportunities.

Lebanese immigrants also came to America in significant numbers from 1880 to 1940. Most of them were from the Mount Lebanon area of Syria, which became the independent country of Lebanon. They intended to make lots of money in America and then return home. Most of them never returned home but continued to work in America as peddlers, selling their wares in isolated areas.

The second wave came after World War II ended in 1945. Lebanese immigrants were often looking for better jobs and tended to settle in cities such as Detroit, New York, and Boston. Some found industrial work, while others worked in professions such as engineering.

The Lebanese brought with them their love of literature, music, and dance. In most Lebanese families, someone plays the **oud**, a pear-shaped instrument like a guitar. Folk music played on the oud accompanies the Lebanese national dance, the **dubke**. Dubke dancers hold hands and form a line or circle. The dubke is popular at dinner dances where the Lebanese Americans like to talk with friends and family and eat.

Lebanese cooking is known for being very tasty and fragrant, containing ingredients such as

- Fruits, including lemons, limes, bananas, melons, peaches, and figs.
- Vegetables, including tomatoes, onions, eggplants, spinach, and garlic.
- Spices, such as brown cumin and cardamom.
- Seafood and meat, including lamb, mutton (sheep), and chicken. Beef is generally not available because cattle can't be grazed in mountains. Also, pork is not available because Muslims cannot eat pork.

Lebanese American cooks buy staples such as honey, rice, dried beans and peas, lentils, and bulgur. **Bulgur** looks like a cereal and is made from wheat kernels that have been steamed, dried, and crushed.

Before meals, Lebanese Americans enjoy a variety of appetizers, called **mezze** in Arabic. Mezze can be hot or cold, and pita bread is used to scoop them up. Pita is a Middle Eastern round, flat bread that forms a pocket when slit open. Typical mezze include eggplant dip, called **baba ghanoush**, and **hummus**, a spread using chickpeas (also called garbanzo beans).

Favorite Lebanese dishes include

- **Kibbeh**: ground lamb mixed with spices and bulgur and baked in a flat pan
- **Mishwi**: meat kabobs, often served with rice
- Chicken with garlic and lemon sauce
- **Tabbouleh**: a salad that includes bulgur, parsley, olive oil, and other tasty ingredients

Most often dessert is fruit, and occasionally pudding is served. Pastries with honey are sometimes eaten between meals and on special occasions.

•••••••••••••••• •••• Hummus Bi-tahini •••• ••••••••••••••••

Time
20 minutes

Tools
can opener
measuring cups
measuring spoons
colander
blender
cutting board
paring knife
cup
medium bowl
potato masher
rubber spatula
serving bowl

Makes
6 servings

The two main ingredients in hummus are chickpeas and **tahini**—*a paste made from sesame seeds. This traditional dip can be served with crackers or flat bread as an appetizer, snack, or part of a meal.*

Ingredients

1 15-ounce can chickpeas
3 lemons
1 garlic clove
1 cup tahini
½ teaspoon salt

2 teaspoons olive oil
¼ teaspoon paprika
1 teaspoon dried parsley
flat bread or water crackers

Steps

1. Open the can of chickpeas and drain into a colander. Rinse chickpeas with cold water.

2. Place all but 3 tablespoons of chickpeas into the blender.

3. Roll the lemons on a flat surface to loosen the membranes. On a cutting board, cut the lemons in half. Squeeze each lemon half so that the juice goes into a cup. Pour the lemon juice into the blender.

4. Peel the papery skin off the garlic clove. Add the garlic clove, tahini, and salt to the blender. Puree the chickpea mixture until smooth.

5. Mash the remaining chickpeas in a medium bowl with a potato masher. Fold the contents of the blender into this bowl using a rubber spatula.

6. Transfer the hummus to a serving bowl.

7. Drizzle the olive oil over the top. Sprinkle with paprika and parsley.

8. Serve with flat bread or water crackers.

Ree's Tabbouleh

Ree's son is a friend of our family. He remembers this salad being a family favorite. Tabbouleh is a well-known salad made with bulgur. The bulgur kernels become bigger when soaked. Bulgur has a nutty flavor and a chewy texture.

Ingredients

1   cup bulgur
1   bunch fresh parsley
1   bunch mint
3   scallions
2   lemons

1   garlic clove
⅓   cup olive oil
½   teaspoon salt
¼   teaspoon pepper
½   cup diced tomatoes

Steps

1. Put the bulgur in a medium bowl with 1 cup of hot water. The bulgur will absorb the water.

2. Wash the parsley and mint leaves in a colander under running water. Roll the herbs in paper towels to dry.

3. Wash the scallions and pat dry. On a cutting board, cut off the roots and slice the white portion into ¼-inch slices. Finely chop the slices and discard the green tops.

4. Roll the lemons on a flat surface to loosen the membranes. Cut the lemons in half. Squeeze each lemon half over a measuring cup until you have ⅓ cup of juice. Remove pits.

5. Peel the papery skin off the garlic clove. Slice the garlic with a paring knife and mince.

6. Combine the scallions, lemon juice, garlic, olive oil, salt, and pepper in a small bowl and whisk together.

7. Fold the lemon juice mixture into the bulgur with a rubber spatula. Add the tomatoes and continue folding.

Time
30 minutes

Tools
measuring cups
measuring spoons
medium bowl
colander
paper towels
cutting board
paring knife
small bowl
whisk
rubber spatula
large serving plate or bowl

Makes
4 servings

8. Take the parsley leaves off the stems, then discard the stems. Gather the parsley into a small ball and slice. Mince the parsley with a knife and continue until you measure ½ cup.

9. Take the mint leaves off the stems. Stack 5 or 6 mint leaves and roll lengthwise. Cut the leaves into ¼-inch slices until you measure ½ cup.

10. Using a rubber spatula, carefully fold the herbs into the bulgur mixture.

11. Place the tabbouleh into a large serving plate or bowl.

CHAPTER 10

MEXICO

Mexico is located between the southwestern United States and Central America. Because Mexico is farther south than the United States, the climate is generally warmer and many crops can be grown.

A number of great civilizations including the Olmec, Maya, and Aztec civilizations, thrived in ancient Mexico. The Olmecs were the first ancient civilization of Mexico, and they were known for their cave painting and statues. The Mayans were master architects and engineers. The Aztecs were a warlike people who built a powerful and rich empire. They also built cities with palaces, parks, zoos, and aqueducts to carry water.

In about 1519, the Spanish explorer Hernando Cortes landed in what is now Mexico, and he soon conquered the Aztecs. Much of the Aztec culture and cuisine, however, lived on in the people who became the Mexicans. Mexico was ruled by Spain until 1821. After the Spanish took over, many native Mexicans moved north into what later became the southwestern United States. The state of Texas was actually part of Mexico until it declared its independence in 1836.

Due to political unrest and widespread poverty, many Mexicans have come to live in the United States since 1900. Many immigrants, including wealthy landowners and government officials, poured into the United States during the Mexican Revolution (1910–1920). Once the Great Depression hit the United States in 1929, many Mexican Americans moved north from the border towns where they had first settled to places such as California and Illinois to find jobs.

In 1942, Mexicans were encouraged to enter the United States for the time needed to help harvest crops, because they worked for less money than Americans. When this program ended in 1964, migrant workers continued to enter the United States, but illegally this time. Today, despite border patrols and high fences, many Mexicans try to illegally cross into the United States to escape poverty and find higher-paying jobs. Trips crossing the border can be very dangerous, as travel frequently involves crossing rivers, deserts, mountains, and dealing with bandits. Not all Mexicans enter illegally. Many do get visas, but they may have to wait up to five years to get one.

Mexicans bring a unique culture to the United States. **Mariachi** music is a traditional form of Mexican music that blends the sounds of brass and string instruments. The **jalisco** is a Mexican folk dance that dates back to the 1700s and is used when a man is dating a woman. The Spanish brought the Catholic religion to Mexico, and this faith is important to many Mexican Americans. Religious holidays, such as Navidad (Christmas), are times for fiestas (or festivals) that feature dancing and singing.

Mexican American cooking reflects the influences of the Spanish and also the native Mexicans. The foods of the native Mexicans included corn, peppers, squash, beans, chocolate, pineapple, avocados, and potatoes. Corn is used to make flour, called *masa harina*, which is used in tortillas. The corn tortilla is a thin, flat pancake that is present at most Mexican American meals. Tortillas are used in a number of dishes.

- **Tacos**: Mexican American tacos use the folded and fried tortillas that are common in the United States. In Mexico, a taco is made from two warm, soft corn tortillas that are stacked, filled, and then folded. The filling for tacos includes meat and/or beans, garnishes, such as chopped lettuce, and salsa, a type of sauce.

- **Quesadillas**: Quesadillas are like grilled cheese sandwiches. To make a quesadilla, you top a tortilla with cheese and other toppings, then fold it in half and cook in a skillet. Turn once or twice and cook until the filling is hot and the cheese is melted. Sometimes quesadillas are cut into wedges for serving.

- **Enchiladas**: Enchiladas are rolled-up tortillas stuffed with fillings. They are baked with sauce and cheese.

- **Burritos**: A burrito consists of a soft flour tortilla that is usually filled with beans and meat and is then rolled up. Burritos are often served with lettuce, tomatoes, salsa, and sour cream. If a burrito is fried, it is called a **chimichanga**.

- **Fajitas**: Fajitas are grilled meat, and possibly grilled vegetables such as green peppers, served on a flour tortilla with condiments such as lettuce, tomatoes, sour cream, and salsa.

Besides tortillas, another staple of Mexican cooking is the chile pepper, which is in the same family as the green bell pepper. Chile peppers have been farmed in Mexico for over 5,000 years. Over a hundred different chile peppers grow in Mexico. They come in different colors, sizes, and flavors. Some chile peppers are sweet, but most are hot, and some are very hot! They have names such as jalapeño or Serrano.

Salsa, a Mexican sauce that is now almost as popular in America as ketchup, is made from chile peppers, tomatoes, onions, garlic, and often additional ingredients. Salsa is served with tacos, enchiladas, and many other dishes.

Other ingredients used in Mexican foods include **jicama**, lime, and cumin. Jicama is a root vegetable. It is brown and has white flesh that is tasty in salads. Mexicans use a different kind of lime, called a "key lime" in English and a *limón* in Spanish. The limón is sweeter than many other limes, and its juice is used in soups, salsas, and other dishes.

Other Mexican dishes introduced to the United States include carne asada and molé chicken. *Carne asada* is grilled meat that was marinated before cooking. To marinate a food is to let it soak in a liquid called a marinade, which flavors and tenderizes the food. *Carne asada* is served with tortillas. What makes *molé* chicken so unique is its sauce that contains a number of ingredients including chiles, peanuts, and chocolate.

True Mexican foods do not normally use the amount of cheese, sour cream, and meat found in many American restaurants. Authentic Mexican foods use lots of fresh fruits, vegetables, rice, beans, and seafood with only small amounts of cheese or meats.

Amazing Avocado Dip

The avocado is a pear-shaped fruit with a large pit, green skin, and yellow-green insides. Guacamole is the Mexican name for avocado dip, and it is served as an appetizer with tortilla chips, as a salad on lettuce, or as a garnish for Mexican dishes.

Ingredients

1 medium onion

1 garlic clove

4 ripened avocados (soft to the touch)

2 tablespoons fresh, chopped cilantro leaves or 2 teaspoons dried cilantro

1 tablespoon lemon juice

1 cup chicken stock

⅛ teaspoon cayenne pepper

1 tablespoon cider vinegar

1 teaspoon salt

6 plum tomatoes

6 large Romaine lettuce leaves

tortilla chips

1 teaspoon dried parsley

Time
20 to 25 minutes

Tools
cutting board
paring knife
spoon
blender
measuring cups
measuring spoons
small bowl
plastic wrap
paper towels
large plate

Makes
6 servings

Steps

1. Remove the papery skin from the onion. On a cutting board, cut the onion in half. Lay the flat sides down and chop into small pieces.

2. Peel the papery skin from the garlic clove. On a cutting board, chop.

3. Cut 2 avocados in half. Pull the avocados apart, and take out the pits. Use a spoon to scoop the avocado flesh (insides) into a blender.

4. Add the onion, garlic, cilantro, lemon juice, chicken stock, cayenne pepper, cider vinegar, and salt to the blender. Puree until the mixture is smooth.

5. Transfer the avocado dip to a small bowl and cover with plastic wrap.

6. Wash the tomatoes and romaine lettuce and pat dry.

7. On a cutting board, cut the plum tomatoes into quarters.

8. Cut the 2 remaining avocados in half. Take out the pits. Use a spoon to remove the skin from the flesh. Lay the avocado flesh flat side down on a cutting board to slice into wedges.

9. Line a large plate with the lettuce leaves. Place the dip in the center of the plate. Then decorate the plate with plum tomatoes, avocado wedges, and tortilla chips. Garnish with parsley.

•••••••••• •••• Oh-So-Hot Salsa •••• ••••••••••

Salsa is another great dip that you can serve along with the Amazing Avocado Dip, or it can be used in the next recipe, Awesome Tex-Mex Spuds.

Ingredients

2 14½-ounce cans diced tomatoes
2 plum tomatoes
1 garlic clove
2 scallions

½ jalapeño pepper
1 bunch fresh cilantro
½ lemon
⅓ cup tomato juice
⅛ teaspoon pepper

Steps

1. Open the cans of diced tomatoes and put the tomatoes in a medium bowl.

2. Wash the plum tomatoes and pat dry. Using a cutting board, cut them into ½-inch slices, then chop. Place them in the bowl with the diced tomatoes.

3. Peel the papery skin off the garlic clove. Using a cutting board, mince the garlic. Place the garlic in the bowl with the tomatoes.

4. Wash the scallions and pat dry. Cut off the roots of the scallions. Chop the white parts only and add to the bowl.

5. Before you cut the jalapeño pepper, put on plastic gloves or cover your hands with sandwich bags so that your skin does not sting from touching it. Be careful not to touch your skin, eyes, or face while working. Cut off the top and bottom of the jalapeño pepper. Remove and discard the ribs and seeds. Chop half the jalapeño pepper and add to the bowl. Thoroughly clean knives and work surfaces when you finish.

6. Wash the cilantro and pat dry. Using kitchen scissors, snip the leaves off the stems. Cut the leaves into smaller pieces until you have ¼ cup. Add to the bowl.

Time
30 minutes to prepare
plus
4 hours to chill

Tools
can opener
medium bowl
paper towels
cutting board
paring knife
plastic gloves or 2 sandwich bags
kitchen scissors
wooden spoon
measuring cups
measuring spoons
plastic wrap

Makes
2½ cups

7. Cut the lemon in half. Squeeze it into the bowl with the salsa. Remove any pits.

8. Add the tomato juice and pepper to the bowl, and combine with a wooden spoon.

9. Cover with plastic wrap and refrigerate for at least 4 hours before serving.

Awesome Tex-Mex Spuds

Texas and Mexico are such close neighbors that their cuisines have melded into dishes that have come to be called Tex-Mex. In this dish, the beef of Texas combines with traditional Mexican ingredients like salsa, potatoes, and tomatoes to make a great dinnertime dish.

Ingredients

4   large baking potatoes

1   tomato

4   scallions

1   tablespoon vegetable oil

1   pound lean ground beef or turkey

1   8-ounce can tomato sauce

1   tablespoon chili powder

1   cup salsa

1   teaspoon salt

1   cup shredded Monterey Jack cheese

Steps

1. Wash the potatoes with a scrub brush. Pat dry with paper towels and pierce with a fork.

2. Cook the potatoes on full power in a microwave for 12 to 15 minutes, until they are tender. Use oven mitts to remove the potatoes from the microwave.

3. Meanwhile, wash and dry the tomato. On a cutting board, cut the tomato in half and chop it into small pieces.

4. Wash the scallions and pat dry. Use a paring knife to cut off the root ends. Cut the white portion and 1 inch of the green tops into ¼-inch slices.

5. Preheat a large frying pan on medium heat for 2 minutes, then add the oil.

6. Crumble the ground beef or turkey into the frying pan.

7. Using a wooden spoon for stirring, cook the meat over medium heat for 8 to 10 minutes, until browned. Turn off the heat and drain the fat into a small container.

Time
30 to 35 minutes

Tools
vegetable scrub brush
paper towels
table fork
oven mitts
cutting board
paring knife
large frying pan
measuring cups
measuring spoons
wooden spoon
can opener
tablespoon
microwave-safe dish

Makes
4 servings

8. Place the frying pan back on the stove. Turn the heat to medium.

9. Open the can of tomato sauce. Add the tomato sauce, scallions, chili powder, salsa, and salt to the meat. Simmer for five minutes, stirring occasionally.

10. When the potatoes are cool enough to handle, cut them in half lengthwise. With a spoon, scoop out about 2 table-spoons of each potato half to form a small well. Place the potatoes on a microwave-safe plate.

11. Spoon the meat mixture equally on each potato half, and top with chopped tomato and cheese.

12. Put the potatoes in the microwave on full power for 1 minute or until the cheese has melted. Serve immediately.

Mexican Bean Salad

Mexicans have brought to the United States a love for a wide variety of beans, such as navy beans and kidney beans. This salad uses several Mexican favorites.

Ingredients

1 15½-ounce can red kidney beans
1 14½-ounce can green beans
1 14-ounce can pinto beans
1 medium onion
2 celery stalks

⅓ cup white vinegar
2 tablespoons olive oil
1 teaspoon chili powder
½ teaspoon cumin
dash cayenne pepper
¼ teaspoon salt

Steps

1. Open the cans of kidney beans, green beans, and pinto beans. Empty all the cans into a colander to drain off the liquid, then put the beans in a medium bowl.

2. Remove the papery skin from the onion. Using a cutting board, cut the onion in half. Lay each onion half flat on the cutting board and chop.

3. Wash the celery stalks. Pat dry with paper towels. Chop off and discard the ends. Thinly slice the celery.

4. Put the chopped onion and sliced celery in the bowl with the beans.

5. In a small bowl, whisk together the vinegar, olive oil, chili powder, cumin, cayenne pepper, and salt to make a dressing.

6. Pour the oil-and-vinegar dressing over the beans.

7. Cover the bowl with plastic wrap and refrigerate the salad for 2 hours before serving.

Time
30 minutes
plus
2 hours to chill

Tools
can opener
colander
medium bowl
cutting board
knife
small bowl
measuring cups
measuring spoons
whisk
plastic wrap

Makes
8 servings

About the size of California, Morocco is located on the northwestern tip of Africa. On a clear day in Morocco, you can see Spain across the Strait of Gibraltar. Morocco has coastlines along both the Atlantic Ocean and the Mediterranean Sea. The African nations of Algeria and Mauritania border Morocco. Along with sandy beaches and some land that can be farmed, Morocco has four mountain ranges and part of the Sahara Desert. The climate is generally warm and dry except in the mountains, where it is quite cold in the winter.

Morocco has been largely occupied by one group throughout history: the Berbers, the original inhabitants. Because of its location close to Europe and at the opening to the Mediterranean Sea, over the years many foreigners came to Morocco to trade, to settle, and, in some cases, to invade. By the eighth century, Arab forces occupied most of North Africa, including what is now Morocco. The Arabs brought their civilization, including their religion, Islam. Morocco's independence ended in 1912 when a treaty gave most of Morocco to France and a small portion of the country to Spain. By 1956, Morocco had regained its independence.

The first wave of Arabs came to America from countries in North Africa and the Middle East from 1880 to 1940. The second wave came after World War II ended in 1945. Arab immigrants were often looking for better jobs and tended to settle in cities such as Detroit, New York, and Boston. Some found industrial work, while others worked in professions such as engineering.

Moroccan culture has been influenced by both the Berbers and the Arabs. Before the Arabs occupied Morocco, the Berbers had developed their own music. Berber music is used to tell stories and pass them on from family to family, and from generation to generation. The Berbers are also known for their dances, such as the *ahidous*, a complex circle dance performed at harvest time. Geometric figures, such as the triangle, are used in much Islamic art, and Moroccan artists have perfected the use of geometrical patterns.

Moroccan immigrants bring with them a rich cuisine including foods such as couscous and tajine. **Couscous** is actually both an ingredient and the name of a dish. Like pasta, couscous is made from wheat flour. Once cooked, it looks like small pieces of golden rice. As a dish, the grain couscous is topped with a rich stew that is spicy and fragrant, but not hot. Couscous is originally a Berber dish, as is tajine. **Tajine** is a stew of meat and vegetables, sometimes with the addition of fruits and nuts. A typical tajine might include lamb with dates, fish with tomatoes, or chicken with preserved lemons and olives. Lamb and chicken are common meats and seafood is also popular. Pork is not eaten, because most Moroccans are Muslim. The original Berber tajines often omitted any meat and included only vegetables and beans or lentils. A flat bread, called **khubz**, is made fresh every morning and served at meals.

Mint tea, a favorite Moroccan beverage, is served before and after meals, as well as for morning or afternoon tea. Sweet pastries, such as coconut cakes or honey pastries, may occasionally be served with tea.

Moroccans enjoy a wide variety of fruits and vegetables. Fruits include many varieties of orange, grapefruits, and lemons as well as melons, olives, plums, apricots, grapes, figs, and dates. Vegetables include potatoes, onions, zucchini, carrots, and pumpkin. Eggplant is a favorite in Morocco and features in many cooked vegetable salads as well as in fried dishes.

Many of the spices used in Moroccan foods were introduced by the Arabs, such as saffron, a spice that has a strong yellow color and a unique taste. Arabs also brought spices such as cinnamon, pepper, and ginger. To this mix, the Moroccans added several they grew themselves: cilantro, parsley, and cumin. With this collection of seasonings, Moroccans do a wonderful job of producing fragrant, spicy (but not fiery hot) dishes.

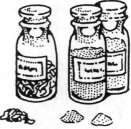

Zuri's Orange-Nut Couscous

Time
40 minutes

Tools
measuring cups
measuring spoons
medium pot with lid
wooden spoon
cutting board
paring knife
large frying pan
large serving bowl
rubber spatula

Makes
4 servings

Zuri is a family friend who contributed this recipe. Couscous is a mainstay of the Moroccan family and has become popular in American cuisine as well. The orange juice and spices used in this recipe are typical of the blend of interesting flavors used in Moroccan foods.

Ingredients

2 cups orange juice	1 medium onion
1 teaspoon cinnamon	1 green pepper
¼ teaspoon cloves	1 tablespoon olive oil
¼ teaspoon tumeric	¼ teaspoon salt
⅓ teaspoon cayenne pepper	¼ teaspoon black pepper
1 package instant couscous	½ cup almond slices
½ cup raisins	

Steps

1. Put the orange juice, cinnamon, cloves, tumeric, and cayenne pepper in a medium pot. Stir with a wooden spoon. Place the pot on medium-high heat to bring the mixture to a boil.

2. Once the orange juice mixture boils, add the couscous and raisins. Stir. Cover the pan and turn off the heat. Let the couscous stand 10 minutes or until the juice is completely absorbed.

3. Meanwhile, remove the papery skin from the onion. Using a cutting board, cut the onion in half. Lay each onion half flat on the cutting board and chop into small pieces.

4. Cut the green pepper in half. Scoop out the seeds and cut the ribs out carefully with a knife, and discard.

5. Lay the peppers flat-side down on the cutting board and cut into strips. Cut the strips into ¼-inch pieces.

6. Preheat a large frying pan over medium heat for 2 minutes. Add the olive oil.

7. When the olive oil is heated up, add the chopped onions and peppers. Cook for 3 to 4 minutes or until tender. Turn off the heat. Cool for 10 minutes.

8. Once the couscous is ready, put it into a large serving bowl. Add the cooled vegetables, salt, and pepper. Mix gently with a rubber spatula.

9. Sprinkle the almond slices over the couscous and serve.

Time
5 minutes

Tools
cutting board
paring knife
measuring cups
measuring spoons
blender
2 tall glasses

Makes
2 servings

Fruit juices and milkshakes helped Moroccans beat the heat in their country. Favorites included orange juice, which usually had sugar added to it, as well as banana milkshakes and even apple milkshakes!

Ingredients

2 bananas

2 cups low-fat or nonfat milk

2 tablespoons sugar

1 teaspoon rosewater or orange flower water (optional)

Steps

1. Peel the bananas. On a cutting board, slice the bananas into 1-inch slices.

2. Put the sliced bananas, milk, sugar, and rosewater or orange flower water into the blender.

3. Blend on high until smooth.

4. Pour into tall glasses and enjoy.

Moroccan Lemon Anise Bread

Moroccans frequently use anise seeds in breads and other baked goods. Anise seeds taste a little like licorice. This bread is delicious with mint tea, the national drink of Morocco.

Ingredients

⅔ cup water

1 teaspoon sugar

1½ teaspoons active dry yeast

1 lemon

1 teaspoon canola oil

2 teaspoons lemon extract

2 cups all-purpose flour

1 teaspoon anise seeds

1 teaspoon salt

vegetable oil cooking spray

1 tablespoon cornmeal

1 egg white

1 teaspoon water

1 tablespoon sesame seeds

Steps

1. Measure ⅔ cup of lukewarm water. Using an instant-read thermometer, check the temperature of the water. Get the temperature to about 110°F.

2. Place the ⅔ cup of water into a small bowl. Using a wooden spoon, stir the sugar into the water until it dissolves.

3. Sprinkle the yeast on top of the water. Set aside for 5 minutes until bubbly.

4. Wash the lemon and pat dry with paper towels.

5. On a piece of waxed paper, use a grater or a zester to remove 1 tablespoon of zest from the lemon. Zest is the colored, outermost layer of skin that has the flavor of the fruit. Do not remove the white part of the skin—it has a bitter taste.

6. Add the oil and lemon extract to the yeast mixture and pour into a large mixing bowl.

Time
20 minutes to prepare
plus
80 minutes to rise
plus
30 minutes to bake

Tools
measuring cups
measuring spoons
instant-read thermometer
2 small bowls
wooden spoon
paper towels
zester or grater
waxed paper
large bowl
medium bowl
kitchen towel
cookie sheet
egg separator
table fork
pastry brush
oven mitts
wire rack

Makes
1 loaf (16 servings)

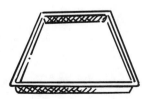

7. Add the lemon zest, flour, anise seeds, and salt to the bowl. Mix vigorously with a wooden spoon until thoroughly combined.

8. On a lightly floured surface, knead the dough by pushing the dough away with the heels of your hands and folding it toward you for about 5 minutes until smooth and silky. Allow the dough to rest for 5 minutes after kneading.

9. Meanwhile, spray a medium mixing bowl with vegetable oil cooking spray. Place the dough in the bowl, turning the dough to coat all sides with the oil.

10. Cover the dough with a kitchen towel and let rise in a warm place for about 70 minutes or until the dough doubles in size.

11. Preheat the oven to 375°F. Spray a baking sheet with vegetable oil cooking spray and sprinkle with cornmeal.

12. Punch down the dough. Shape it into a circle and flatten into a disk with your hands. Let the dough rest for 10 minutes.

13. Separate the egg with an egg separator over a small bowl. Add 1 teaspoon of water to the egg white and beat with a fork. Discard the yolk or freeze for another use.

14. Brush the bread with the egg white and sprinkle with sesame seeds. Place on the cookie sheet.

15. Use oven mitts to place in oven. Bake for 30 minutes or until golden brown and hollow-sounding when tapped with your finger.

16. Using oven mitts, take the bread out of the oven and transfer to a wire rack.

CHAPTER 12
THE NETHERLANDS

The Kingdom of the Netherlands (sometimes called Holland) is a country in northern Europe bordered by the North Sea, Germany, and Belgium. Netherlands means "low land," and indeed one-quarter of the country lies below sea level. The Dutch, the people of the Netherlands, dammed waterways, drained many lakes and marshes, filled them with earth, and built houses, farms, and businesses on the land. About one-third of this land became pastureland, and there are many cows in the pastures. Dams still help keep much of the Netherlands from flooding. Windmills use the wind to power pumps, which also help to keep the drained lands free of water. The Netherlands has a mild, damp climate, and farmers grow vegetables, such as potatoes, and fruits, such as apples. The Dutch are well known for growing beautiful flowers, particularly tulips.

The Dutch were among the earliest settlers in the American colonies. By 1624, a fur-trading post built by the Dutch above New York City became part of a colony called New Netherland. Two years later, New Amsterdam, a settlement on Manhattan Island (the center of New York City), was started. The names of other Dutch settlements still exist today, such as Harlem, which is named after the Dutch town of Haarlem. In 1664, the English defeated the Dutch and took over their American settlement.

Very few Dutch came again to America until the 1840s. A number of problems caused the rise in immigration: crop failures, a revolt against the Dutch Reformed Church, heavy taxes, and poor economic conditions. As the Dutch economy improved into the early 1900s, fewer Dutch immigrated to America until after World War II. After the war, the Dutch economy was in ruins, which spurred some to come to America. Since 1968, their country has enjoyed more prosperous times, and few Dutch have immigrated.

The early Dutch settlers stayed mostly in New York, New Jersey, and Pennsylvania. Later immigrants settled mostly in Midwestern states, such as Michigan, Wisconsin, and Illinois. These immigrants often settled in neighborhoods where they established associations to maintain their ethnic and religious ties.

The Netherlands is famous for its cheeses, such as Gouda and Edam. Gouda and Edam are named after the towns in which they are made. These cheeses are readily available in the United States.

The Dutch brought to America a number of foods that we commonly eat for breakfast, including pancakes, waffles, and doughnuts. Dutch doughnuts were deep-fried balls of dough. Later on, the shape changed to the traditional circle with a hole in the middle. The Dutch also brought over a cabbage salad that became what we now call coleslaw.

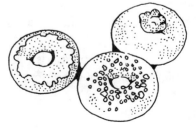

···· Dutch Stew ····

With traditional Dutch stew, called Hutsput, meats and vegetables are cooked together in liquid. Then the vegetables are mashed, and the meat and gravy are put on top of the vegetables. In this Americanized version, the vegetables are not mashed and the stew is simply served on egg noodles.

Ingredients

1   medium onion
2   large baking potatoes
3   tablespoons olive oil
1   pound cubed braising beef
1   cup water
1   teaspoon salt

½   teaspoon pepper
1   Dutch smoked sausage (or any smoked sausage)
1   10½ ounce package frozen carrots
½   pound egg noodles

Time

30 minutes to prepare
plus
2 hours to cook

Tools

cutting board
paring knife
vegetable peeler
large frying pan with lid
or Dutch oven
measuring cups
measuring spoons
wooden spoon
serving bowl
ladle

Makes

6 servings

Steps

1. Remove the outer, papery skin from the onion. Using a cutting board, cut each onion in half. Place each onion half on the cutting board and chop.

2. Peel the potatoes. Cut the potatoes in half, then cut into 1-inch cubes.

3. Preheat a large frying pan or Dutch oven on medium heat for 2 minutes. Add the olive oil.

4. Add the beef and cook, stirring constantly with a wooden spoon for about 5 minutes or until browned.

5. Add the water to the frying pan or Dutch oven and simmer the meat, covered, for 1 hour.

6. Add the onions, potatoes, salt, and pepper. Cover and continue simmering for an additional 45 minutes.

7. Slice the smoked sausage.

8. Finish the stew by adding the sausage and carrots. Continue cooking, uncovered, for 15 minutes.

9. Cook ½ pound dried egg noodles according to the package instructions. Place in a serving bowl.

10. Ladle the stew over the egg noodles.

Dutch Apple Cake

The Dutch are well known for their apple cake, which is popular in America as well.

Ingredients

vegetable oil cooking spray
2 medium apples
1½ cups all-purpose flour
1 tablespoon baking powder
¼ teaspoon salt
¼ cup sugar

¼ cup margarine
1 egg
¾ cup low-fat or nonfat milk
2 tablespoons sugar
½ teaspoon ground cinnamon

Steps

1. Preheat the oven to 400°F.
2. Spray an 8 × 8-inch baking pan with vegetable oil cooking spray.
3. Wash the apples and pat dry with paper towels.
4. Peel the apples. Using a cutting board, cut the apples in half and remove the seeds. Cut each apple half into 4 wedges.
5. In a large bowl, stir together the flour, baking powder, salt, and ¼ cup of sugar with a wooden spoon.
6. Cut the margarine into the flour mixture with the pastry blender, using a back-and-forth motion until the mixture looks like small peas.
7. Break the egg into a small bowl and beat with a fork. Add the milk and mix.
8. Add the egg and milk mixture to the flour mixture. Stir well.
9. Pour the batter into the baking pan.

Time
25 minutes to prepare
plus
30 minutes to bake

Tools
8 × 8-inch baking pan
paper towels
vegetable peeler
cutting board
paring knife
large bowl
measuring cups
measuring spoons
wooden spoon
pastry blender
2 small bowls
table fork
oven mitts

Makes
8 servings

10. Press the apple wedges partly into the batter.

11. In a small bowl, combine 2 tablespoons of sugar and cinnamon. Sprinkle over the apples.

12. Use oven mitts to put pan in oven. Bake for 25 to 30 minutes until golden brown. Remove from oven with oven mitts.

Dutch Windmill Cookies

At Christmas time, the Dutch have traditionally made cookies in the shapes of windmills, farm animals, and other reminders of daily life. Today, you can also find these spicy windmill cookies in America.

Ingredients

vegetable oil cooking spray

1 cup margarine

1½ cups brown sugar

1 egg

2¾ cups all-purpose flour

1 teaspoon baking powder

¼ teaspoon salt

1½ teaspoons cinnamon

½ teaspoon ground nutmeg

½ teaspoon ground cloves

½ cup sliced almonds

2 tablespoons flour for rolling cookies

Steps

1. Preheat the oven to 350°F.

2. Spray cookie sheets with vegetable oil cooking spray.

3. In a medium bowl, beat the margarine, brown sugar, and egg with an electric mixer for 3 minutes on medium speed until fluffy.

4. Turn the mixer off. Add the flour, baking powder, salt, cinnamon, nutmeg, and cloves to the bowl. Mix thoroughly with a wooden spoon.

5. Place ⅓ cup of the sliced almonds in a zipper-lock bag. Close the bag and crush the almonds with a rolling pin by rolling it back and forth. Fold the almond into the cookie dough with a rubber spatula.

6. On a lightly floured surface, roll the dough with a floured rolling pin until the dough is about ½ inch thick.

7. Cut the dough into windmill (or other) shapes using cookie cutters.

Time
30 minutes to prepare
plus
30 minutes to bake

Tools
2 cookie sheets
measuring cups
measuring spoons
medium bowl
hand-held electric mixer
wooden spoon
zipper-lock plastic bag
rolling pin
rubber spatula
windmill cookie cutters (or other shapes)
oven mitts
spatula
wire rack

Makes
4 dozen cookies

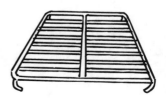

8. Place the cookies 2 inches apart on a cookie sheet. Decorate with the remaining sliced almonds.

9. Use oven mitts to place in oven. Bake for 8 to 10 minutes or until lightly browned. Using oven mitts, remove from the oven.

10. Let the cookies cool on the cookie sheet for 1 minute. Remove with a spatula and transfer to a wire rack to finish cooling.

11. Repeat steps 9 and 10 until all cookies are baked.

 IGERIA

Nigeria is a country in western Africa. The countries of Benin, Niger, Chad, and Cameroon are its neighbors. Nigeria lies on the Gulf of Guinea and has a coastal plain that allows for farming. As you move north from the coastal plain, there are plateaus and small mountains. The climate is hot, and most of the rain comes during one rainy season.

Nigeria has more people than any other country in Africa. There are over 250 ethnic groups and tribes and many religions. The three main ethnic groups are the Hausa in the north, the Ibo in the east, and the Yoruba in the west. The conflicts between Nigeria's ethnic groups and tribes have created problems, including violence, for many years. This has caused some Nigerians to come to the United States to work and/or get an education.

Nigerians arrived in the United States as early as the 1600s, not as free people but as slaves. From the 17th through the 19th centuries, European traders established ports for slave traffic along the West African coast. There were ports in Nigeria where Africans were loaded like cattle onto ships for long, dangerous trips to the Americas. Once they arrived in America, the Africans were put to work on farms and plantations, mainly in the South. Slaves from Nigeria were forced to give up much of their homeland culture, but some things remained and became part of American culture.

After 1900, immigration from Africa to America increased, as slavery had been outlawed for over 30 years. Immigration slowed down from 1924 to 1965, when laws limited the number of immigrants from Africa. Now, the majority of Africans who come to America are from Nigeria. Most Africans who have arrived here in the last 20 years have come to better themselves through good-paying jobs and better education.

Nigerian culture has a rich and long tradition of art, music, and writing. Nigerian art goes back more than 2,000 years and includes carved sculptures and masks, as well as paintings. *Yoruba* masks are carved out of wood and represent the forces of nature and gods. African *juju* music began in Nigeria and uses guitars, African drums, and complex harmonies. Many Nigerian authors, such as Chinua Achebe, tell fascinating stories that are read around the world.

In addition to their culture, Nigerians also brought to America a taste for familiar foods such as the following:

- Jollof rice: **Jollof rice** is a typical main dish that combines vegetables, such as tomatoes and peppers, a starch, such as rice, and meat or fish (if available) into a one-pot meal.

- Fufu: **Fufu** is a starchy accompaniment to stews and other dishes with sauces. Traditional fufu is made with pounded yams or plantains. Fufu is served on a plate at the table, and diners roll up pieces of fufu with their fingers and use it to scoop up stew or another dish.

- Dodo or boli: Dodo and boli are two ways Nigerians eat plantains. Plantains look like bananas but are not eaten raw. They are flavorful when cooked but never as sweet as a ripe banana. **Dodo** is fried plantains and **boli** is baked plantains. They are both popular snacks, along with fried yam chips. Palm oil is a distinctly Nigerian oil used to fry foods. Made from palm kernels, palm oil has a red color.

Popular fruits include oranges, grapefruits, tangerines, bananas, melons, guava, and limes. Carrots, peppers, tomatoes, okra, spinach, onions, peas, and yams are favorite vegetables. Yams are like sweet potatoes, but they are not as sweet, and they are yellow inside instead of deep orange.

Sausage Roll

Sausage rolls are a popular Nigerian snack food. Try these as a snack or for breakfast.

Time
30 minutes

Tools
large frying pan with lid
tongs
paper towels
measuring spoons
pizza cutter
cookie sheet
small bowl
table fork
pastry brush
oven mitts

Makes
16 small sausage rolls

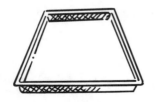

Ingredients

16 frozen breakfast link sausages, fully cooked

2 tablespoons all-purpose flour

1 10-ounce package refrigerated pizza dough

vegetable oil cooking spray

1 egg

2 teaspoons water

Steps

1. Preheat the oven to 425°F.

2. Place the sausage links in a large frying pan. Cover with cold water. Bring to a boil, then reduce heat, cover, and simmer for 6 minutes.

3. Use tongs to remove the sausages and put them on paper towels.

4. Put the flour on a flat, clean surface. Unroll the pizza dough onto the floured surface.

5. Roll the dough into a 16-inch square. Use a pizza cutter to cut the dough into quarters. Then divide each quarter into 4 even squares.

6. Place a sausage on a square of dough and roll up the dough around the biscuit. Continue with the rest of the sausages.

7. Spray a cookie sheet with vegetable oil cooking spray.

8. Arrange the sausage rolls on the cookie sheet.

9. Break the egg into a small bowl and beat with a fork. Add the water.

10. Using a pastry brush, brush the sausage rolls with the egg.

11. Bake for 8 to 12 minutes or until golden.

12. Use oven mitts to remove the sausages from the oven. Let cool for 5 minutes before serving.

•••• Mashed Yams ••••

Time
20 minutes to prepare
plus
40 minutes to cook

Tools
paper towels
vegetable peeler
large frying pan with lid
or Dutch oven
measuring spoons
cutting board
paring knife
table fork
oven mitts
colander
potato masher
wooden spoon
serving bowl

Makes
4 servings

Yams are a staple food in Nigeria and they are prepared in different ways depending on the region. They may be boiled, fried, or pounded into a powder that is then boiled. Try this African American version.

Ingredients

4 large yams
2 teaspoons salt
½ teaspoon pepper
3 tablespoons low-fat or nonfat milk

½ teaspoon nutmeg
3 tablespoons margarine
2 teaspoons dried parsley

Steps

1. Wash the yams and pat dry with paper towels, then peel them.

2. Fill a large frying pan or Dutch oven with water. Bring the water to a boil on high heat. Add 1 teaspoon of salt when the water is boiling.

3. Meanwhile, on a cutting board, cut the yams into ½-inch slices. Cut each slice in half.

4. Carefully drop the yam slices into the boiling water. Turn the heat to low. Cover the yams and simmer for 40 minutes or until tender when pierced with a fork.

5. Using oven mitts, drain the yams into a colander. Return the yams to the pot.

6. With a potato masher, mash the yams until smooth. Add 1 teaspoon salt, pepper, milk, nutmeg, and margarine to the yams and stir with a wooden spoon.

7. Put the yams into a serving bowl and garnish with dried parsley.

CHAPTER 14
NORWAY

The neighboring countries of Norway, Sweden, and Denmark make up the region of northwestern Europe called Scandinavia. This was once the home of the Vikings, who were famous for sailing in long wooden ships. They were great explorers and even sailed as far as North America before Columbus, but their settlements didn't survive. Norway stretches the farthest north of the Scandinavian countries, and about one-third of the country is above the Arctic Circle. Norway is well known for its fjords. A **fjord** is a part of the sea that goes inland from the coast and has steep slopes going up from the water. Because the warm waters of the Gulf Stream sweep the Norwegian coast, much of Norway is not as cold or snowy as you might expect. But with its many mountains, forests, and lakes, only a small amount of Norway's land can be farmed.

The population of Norway grew so fast between 1800 and 1850 that good farmland was very scarce. Many Norwegian families came to America because of the promise of cheap land. Many single men who left Norway later in the 1800s were drawn to the higher wages they could earn in America and to the fact that they would have the right to vote. At the time, only a small elite group could vote in Norway. A small number of Norwegians came to America for religious freedom.

After a long, hard journey across the Atlantic Ocean, most Norwegians endured another long trip to arrive at the open farmland of the Midwest. Over time, Norwegian farmers built big farms and communities in Wisconsin, Minnesota, Iowa, North Dakota, South Dakota, and other Midwest states. Many started their life in America living in sod houses on the prairie, where they were plagued by prairie fires, locusts, droughts, and hot summers. Eventually, Norwegians spread out to states beyond the prairies.

Norwegians brought to America their traditional folk art and music. **Rosemaling** is the decorative folk painting of Norway that began about 1750. This art involves painting flowers on wooden home furnishings, such as tables, chairs, and trunks. Many colors are used, including yellow, blue, blue-green, dull reds, red-orange, and green.

In Norway, much more fish is eaten than meat. Cod is the basis for many meals. Popular fish and meat dishes include poached or baked fish with boiled potatoes, meat cakes (like meat balls) with boiled potatoes and peas, sausage patties with mashed rutabagas, and lamb and cabbage stew.

Grains like wheat, rye, and oats are used to make breads, such as Norwegian flat bread. Norwegians eat many kinds of berries, from strawberries to cloudberries—an orange berry that grows in mountains in Norway close to the clouds. Norwegians are also famous for their waffles, which are often cooked in a heart shape and served with jam or berries and/or whipped cream.

The favorite lunch food is an open-faced sandwich. To make this type of sandwich, you spread butter or mayonnaise on a slice of bread. Next, you top the bread with a lettuce leaf, then a piece of meat, fish, eggs, or cheese. A small slice of lemon or green pepper is then placed on top as a garnish.

Norway has two very old food traditions that were brought to America: the smorgasbord and porridge. It is thought that perhaps the Vikings invented the smorgasbord when they returned from foreign lands with new foods. A **smorgasbord** is a buffet of many dishes from which guests can taste a little of each item. A smorgasbord in America includes hot and cold meats, fish, cheeses, salads, vegetables, breads, and desserts. Porridge has a long history in Norway, and rice porridge (like rice pudding) is eaten for breakfast. A sour cream porridge is common on many holidays and special occasions such as weddings and birthdays. It is made with flour, milk, sour cream, cinnamon, and sugar.

Open-Faced Roast Beef Sandwich

Time
15 minutes

Tools
broiler pan
spreader
oven mitts
spatula
4 plates

Makes
4 open-faced
sandwiches

The traditional Norwegian method for making open-faced sandwiches is still found in America, along with many variations such as this one!

Ingredients

4   slices whole-wheat, rye, or white bread

4   tablespoons Thousand Island dressing

8   thin slices roast beef

4   slices provolone or American cheese

4   tomato slices

Steps

1. Preheat the broiler.

2. Lay the bread out on the broiler pan.

3. Spread 1 tablespoon of dressing on each bread slice.

4. Lay 2 slices of roast beef and then 1 slice of cheese and 1 tomato on top of each bread slice.

5. Use oven mitts to put the broiler pan under the broiler until the cheese melts, about 1 to 2 minutes.

6. Using oven mitts, remove the broiler pan.

7. Use a spatula to remove the open-faced sandwiches to plates. Serve immediately.

Norwegian Waffles

Norwegian waffles are a favorite both in Norway and America. Use this waffle mix to make a wonderful breakfast treat!

Ingredients

vegetable oil (for waffle maker)

2 cups flour

2 tablespoons sugar

¼ teaspoon salt

¼ teaspoon cardamom or cinnamon

3 eggs

1¾ cups low-fat or nonfat milk

4 tablespoons vegetable oil

maple syrup

Steps

1. Lightly oil the waffle maker. Preheat.

2. In a medium bowl, use a wooden spoon to mix the flour, sugar, salt, and cardamom or cinnamon.

3. In another medium bowl, beat the eggs with a fork. Add the milk and vegetable oil and mix well.

4. Add the egg mixture all at once to the dry mixture. Stir just until moistened.

5. Pour about 1 cup of batter on the grids of the preheated, lightly oiled waffle maker. Close the lid quickly. Bake according to manufacturer's directions.

6. When done, use a fork to lift the waffle out. Repeat with the remaining batter. Serve warm with hot maple syrup.

Time

20 to 30 minutes

Tools

waffle maker
2 medium bowls
measuring cups
measuring spoons
wooden spoon
2 table forks

Makes

12 to 14 4-inch waffles

···· Shilling Bun ····

Time
30 minutes to prepare
plus
1½ hours to rise
plus
20 minutes to bake

Tools
measuring cups
measuring spoons
4 small bowls
instant-read thermometer
microwave-safe dish
with lid
medium bowl
wooden spoon
large bowl
kitchen towel
egg separator
table fork
cookie sheet
rolling pin
pastry brush
cutting board
serrated knife
oven mitts
wire rack
whisk

Makes
1 dozen

Long ago, a shilling bun cost a shilling, the Norwegian unit for money. These cinnamon buns are a great addition to a hot and hearty breakfast.

Ingredients

1 cup milk
1 package active dry yeast
4 tablespoons (½ stick) margarine
3½ cups all-purpose flour
½ cup sugar
vegetable oil cooking spray
¼ cup cinnamon

¼ cup sugar
1 egg white
1 teaspoon water
¼ cup confectioner's sugar
2 tablespoons low-fat or nonfat milk
1 teaspoon vanilla extract

Steps

1. In a microwave on full power, heat the milk in a small bowl for about 60 seconds or until it reads 110°F with an instant-read thermometer.

2. Sprinkle the yeast over the milk. Set aside for 5 minutes until the mixture becomes bubbly.

3. In a covered microwave-safe dish, melt the margarine in the microwave on full power for about 60 seconds or until liquid.

4. In a medium bowl, combine the flour and ½ cup of sugar.

5. Add the milk mixture and melted margarine to the flour mixture and beat thoroughly with a wooden spoon until well combined.

6. Turn the dough onto a lightly floured surface. Knead the dough for 5 minutes by pushing the dough away with the heels of your hands and then folding it toward you until it gets silky and smooth.

7. Spray a large bowl with vegetable oil cooking spray.

Place the dough into the bowl and cover with a kitchen towel. Let the dough rise in a draft-free place for 1 hour.

8. Combine the cinnamon and ¼ cup of sugar in a small bowl.

9. Over a small bowl, separate the egg yolk from the egg white. Discard the yolk. Add the water to the egg white and beat with a fork.

10. Spray a cookie sheet with vegetable oil cooking spray.

11. Punch the dough down by pulling the dough up on all sides, folding it over the center, and pressing down.

12. On a lightly floured surface, roll the dough with a rolling pin into a 12 × 15-inch rectangle.

13. Brush the dough with half of the beaten egg white and sprinkle with half the cinnamon sugar.

14. Roll the dough lengthwise into a jellyroll shape. Place on a cookie sheet and refrigerate for 10 minutes.

15. Take the dough out of the refrigerator and brush with the egg white. Sprinkle on the remaining cinnamon sugar.

16. Using a cutting board, cut the dough into 1-inch slices with a serrated knife. Place the buns 1 inch apart on the cookie sheet and cover with a kitchen towel.

17. Let rise for 20 minutes.

18. Preheat the oven to 350°F.

19. Use oven mitts to put the cookie sheet in the oven. Bake for 18 to 20 minutes until puffy and lightly golden brown on top. Use oven mitts to remove from the oven. Let pan cool on a wire rack.

20. In another small bowl, whisk the confectioner's sugar, milk, and vanilla extract together. Drizzle over the cinnamon buns while they are warm. Serve.

CHAPTER 15

POLAND

Poland is a country in eastern Europe. Northern Poland borders the Baltic Sea and Russia. The countries of Lithuania, Belarus, Ukraine, Slovakia, Czech Republic, and Germany also border Poland. Poland, which means "plains" in Polish, is mostly flat; the central plains provide excellent farmlands. The summers are warm and the winters are cold.

Many Poles left their country or were forced to leave in the late 1700s when neighboring countries took control of the land and its people. However, the number of Poles who came to America in the late 1700s was small compared to the over two million Poles who came between 1870 and 1914. Many of these Poles were called "for bread" immigrants because they were very poor and were lacking some of the basic necessities, such as bread. Some had been forced off their farms by the increasingly mechanized agriculture of Europe. The poor farmers and unskilled workers could not compete with the rich for the land. Some of the Poles who came to America were Jewish and left Poland to avoid the resentment and hatred directed at Jews in the early 20th century.

Some Polish immigrants did continue farming in the midwestern and western United States. Many others found work in the meatpacking, steel, and mining industries in eastern and midwestern cities such as Pittsburgh, Chicago, and St. Louis.

When the German Nazi dictator, Adolf Hitler, invaded and took over Poland in 1939, this event sparked World War II. Before and during World War II, the battles and bombings caused many Poles to leave the country. Many also left to escape the brutal Nazis, who killed many Poles, especially Jewish Poles. After World War II ended in 1945, Poland became a communist country. Communism is a system of government in which property is not owned by individuals but is shared by the community. Many Poles at that time came to America to escape communism and find freedom and jobs. In 1989, Poland became a democratic country.

Two of Poland's cultural contributions to the world have been literature and music. Poland's greatest composer was Frederic Chopin, who wrote classical music for the piano. Folk music is very much alive in Poland and was brought to the United States. It is often played to accompany traditional dances such as the **mazur**.

In addition to their culture, the Poles brought over their cooking style and favorite foods. You can see the influence of neighboring countries in some of their dishes, such as goulash (a stew dish) from Hungary, sausage from Germany, and borscht (beet and beef soup) from Russia.

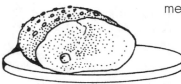

Polish food is often quite hearty. Pork is the most important meat, and the high quality of Polish hams is known around the world. Poles also enjoy over 90 kinds of sausage, called kielbasa. Cabbage and beets are two favorite Polish vegetables. Other popular vegetables include mushrooms and carrots. Pickled vegetables are an essential part of

Polish cooking. Long ago, people would pickle vegetables to preserve them. To pickle a vegetable, a solution of salt and/or vinegar is used. Pickled beets, pickled cabbage (sauerkraut), and even pickled herring are popular foods.

Rye bread is served at many meals. Barley is popular in soups and other dishes. Wheat is used in the dough to make **pierogies**. They are filled with meat, cheese, sauerkraut, mushrooms, or other fillings, then boiled like ravioli.

Traditional Polish desserts include apple cake, doughnuts, and poppy seed rolls. Poppy seed rolls have a filling of poppy seeds, butter, sugar, raisins, almonds, and honey.

Mildred Goldberg's Amazing Stuffed Cabbage Rolls

Time
45 minutes to prepare
plus
1 hour 15 minutes to cook

Tools
large pot
paper towels
cutting board
paring knife
tongs
colander
large frying pan
measuring cups
measuring spoons
can opener
wooden spoon
2 large bowls
spatula
large baking dish
aluminum foil
oven mitts

Makes
8 servings

Mildred Goldberg is a family friend. Mildred's daughter recalls that when her mother used to cook this inexpensive eastern European dish, savory smells would permeate the rooms of their tiny apartment. Truly a crowd-pleaser and a family favorite.

Ingredients

8 large cabbage leaves	½ teaspoon pepper
2 medium onions	all-purpose flour (for coating the cabbage rolls)
1 tablespoon vegetable oil	1 tablespoon vegetable oil
2 pounds lean ground beef	1 quart tomato juice
1 15-ounce can tomato sauce	1 15-ounce can tomato sauce
2 eggs	1 cup sugar
½ cup uncooked rice	1 cup dark raisins
1 teaspoon salt	

Steps

1. Fill a large pot half full with water. Place the pot on the stove on high heat.

2. While the water builds up to a boil, wash the cabbage leaves and pat dry with paper towels. On a cutting board, cut out the center vein from the cabbage leaves by cutting around it in a long V shape. Keep each cabbage leaf in 1 piece.

3. Once the water boils, use tongs to drop 4 leaves at a time into the boiling water. After 2 to 3 minutes, use the tongs to remove the cabbage leaves and drain them well in a colander.

4. Repeat step 3 with the next 4 leaves.

5. Remove the papery skin from the onions. On a cutting board, cut the onions in half. Place the flat sides down, and chop each onion half into small pieces.

6. Preheat a large frying pan on medium heat for 2 minutes, then add the vegetable oil.

7. Add the onions to the frying pan. Sauté for 2 to 3 minutes. Put the onions in a large bowl and set the frying pan aside as it will be used again.

8. Add the ground beef, 1 can of tomato sauce, eggs, rice, salt, and pepper to the onions. Mix well with a wooden spoon.

9. Divide the filling among the 8 cabbage leaves. Place the filling in the center of each cabbage leaf.

10. Fold three sides of the cabbage leaf over the meat mixture so that it resembles an envelope with the top flap open. Starting with the top flap, roll the cabbage leaf, making sure the folded sides are included in the roll.

11. Repeat the previous step until all of the cabbage rolls are made.

12. Lightly flour both sides of the cabbage rolls.

13. Preheat the oven to 350°F.

14. Heat 1 tablespoon of vegetable oil in the large frying pan over medium heat. Use a spatula to place the cabbage rolls in the pan. Brown lightly on both sides for 3 to 4 minutes, then place in a large baking dish.

15. In a large mixing bowl, mix the tomato juice, the second can of tomato sauce, sugar, and raisins with a wooden spoon. Pour over the cabbage rolls.

16. Cover the cabbage rolls with aluminum foil and bake for 1 hour. Uncover and continue cooking for 15 minutes longer.

17. Use oven mitts to remove from the oven. To serve, place the cabbage rolls on plates and spoon some of the sauce from the pan over them.

Time

45 minutes

Tools

measuring cups
measuring spoons
medium bowl
can opener
wooden spoon
cutting board
small bowl
table fork
rolling pin
drinking glass or cookie cutter (about 3 inches in diameter)
large pot or Dutch oven
slotted spoon

Makes

6 servings

In Italy it is called pasta, and in Asia it is called noodles. The Polish version of flour and egg dough is called pierogies. Pierogies can be purchased today in any supermarket and are delicious, with many different fillings and variations.

Ingredients

Dough

2   cups all-purpose flour

2   eggs

½ cup water

½ teaspoon salt

Fillings

Cinnamon and Cheese Filling

1   cup low-fat cottage cheese

1   egg

3   tablespoons sugar

3   tablespoons currants or raisins

½ teaspoon cinnamon

Savory Cheese Filling

1   cup low-fat cottage cheese

1   teaspoon lemon juice

1   egg

1   teaspoon dried parsley

½ teaspoon salt

¼ teaspoon pepper

Sauerkraut-n-Dogs Filling

2   cups sauerkraut

1   hot dog cut into bite-sized pieces

Mushroomy Filling

1   small can button mushrooms, drained

1   chopped onion

1   egg

1   teaspoon dried parsley

½ teaspoon salt

¼ teaspoon pepper

Steps

1. Pick a filling for your pierogies. In a medium bowl, mix the filling ingredients together with a wooden spoon. Set aside.

2. To make the dough, mound the flour on a cutting board and make a hole in the center.

3. Break the eggs into a small bowl and beat with a fork.

4. Add the eggs, water, and salt to the hole. With a fork, stir the flour into the egg mixture until it forms a dough.

5. Knead the dough for about 5 minutes until it is firm. Knead by pressing the dough out with the heel of your hand, then folding it toward you. Give the dough a quarter turn after each fold and start again.

6. When finished kneading, divide the dough in half. Flatten each half into a disk shape. Let rest for 5 minutes.

7. Roll each dough half with a rolling pin onto a lightly floured surface. Roll until the dough is about $\frac{1}{8}$ inch thick.

8. With a drinking glass or cookie cutter, cut out rounds of dough about 3 inches in diameter.

9. Fill a large pot or Dutch oven about three-quarters full with water. Bring to a boil over high heat.

10. Meanwhile, moisten the edges of the dough with a little water. Then place a tablespoon of filling to one side of each dough round. Fold the dough over the filling and press the edges together. Press down around the border of the dough with a fork to keep each pierogie closed up.

11. Use a slotted spoon to gently drop the pierogies into the boiling water.

12. Cook for 3 to 5 minutes or until the pierogies float. Remove with the slotted spoon and serve immediately.

Orange-Iced Babka

Time
30 minutes to make
dough
plus
3 hours to rise
plus
35 minutes to bake

Tools
measuring cups
measuring spoons
instant-read thermometer
microwave-safe cup
paper towels
waxed paper
grater or zester
egg separator
small bowl
small microwave-safe dish
with lid
2 large bowls
2 wooden spoons
kitchen towel
9-inch tube pan
oven mitts
wire rack
small pot
pastry brush

Makes
12 servings

The babka cake originated in eastern Europe and was brought to the United States by early Polish immigrants who settled in Brooklyn, New York. **Babka** *is a sweet yeast cake made with raisins.*

Ingredients

¼ cup water
1 package active-dry yeast
¾ cup low-fat or nonfat milk
1 orange
3 egg yolks
½ cup margarine (1 stick)
1½ cups all-purpose flour
¼ cup sugar
½ teaspoon salt

2½ cups all-purpose flour
¼ cup sugar
vegetable oil cooking spray
1 cup raisins

Icing
¼ cup sugar
2 tablespoons orange juice
¼ cup water

Steps

1. Measure ¼ cup of warm water and use an instant-read thermometer to make sure it is 100–110°F. Sprinkle the yeast on top of the water.

2. Heat the milk in the microwave on high power for about 1 minute or until it reaches about 130°F. Set aside.

3. Wash the orange and dry with paper towels. On a piece of waxed paper, use a grater or a zester to remove 1 teaspoon of zest from the orange. Zest is the colored, outermost layer of skin that has the flavor of the fruit. (Do not remove the white part of the skin—it has a bitter taste.) Set the zest aside.

4. Use an egg separator to separate the egg yolks into a small bowl. Discard the egg whites or freeze for another use.

5. Cut the margarine into small pieces, put in a small microwave-safe dish with a lid, and heat in the microwave at full power for about 20 seconds or until soft.

6. In a large mixing bowl, combine the orange zest, 1½ cups of flour, ¼ cup of sugar, salt, and the dissolved yeast with a wooden spoon.

7. Gradually add the warm milk to the mixture. Thoroughly mix.

8. Slowly add the egg yolks, margarine, 2½ cups of flour, and ¼ cup of sugar. Stir the mixture vigorously with a wooden spoon for about 3 minutes until the dough is smooth and well combined.

9. Spray a large bowl with vegetable oil cooking spray. Place the dough into the bowl and cover with a kitchen towel. Put the bowl in a draft-free place and allow the dough to rise for about 1 hour or until it is almost doubled in size.

10. When you can poke your finger in the dough without the dough springing back, it has doubled in size. Pull the dough up on all sides, fold it over the center, and press down.

11. Spray a 9-inch tube pan with vegetable oil cooking spray.

12. On a lightly floured surface, flatten the dough and fold in the raisins.

13. Place the dough in the tube pan and cover with the kitchen towel. Allow the cake to rise in a draft-free place for about 2 hours or until the dough almost reaches the top of the pan.

14. Preheat the oven to 325°F.

15. Use oven mitts to place in the oven. Bake the babka for 30 to 35 minutes or until golden brown. With oven mitts, remove the cake from the oven. Place on a wire rack to cool for 10 minutes. Then remove the cake from the pan by holding upside down over a plate.

16. Let the cake cool while you make the icing.

17. To prepare the icing, add the sugar, orange juice, and water to a small pot and stir with a wooden spoon. Place the saucepan on the stove over medium heat. Bring the mixture to a boil. Reduce the heat to low and simmer for about 5 minutes, stirring constantly. The icing will resemble a syrup.

18. Brush the warm cake with orange icing using a pastry brush. Let the cake cool completely before serving.

 SOUTH KOREA

The Korean peninsula juts out into the Yellow Sea and the Sea of Japan. Japan is only 124 miles away from Korea. Much of the Korean peninsula is covered with hills and mountains, while the coastline and the rivers provide flatter land for farming. Korea enjoys four seasons. For over 1,000 years, the Korean peninsula was ruled as one country. But since the end of World War II in 1945, two countries have existed: North Korea and South Korea.

Almost all immigrants to America came from South Korea. North Korea is a communist country, and virtually no one is allowed to leave there. Few immigrants left South Korea until 1965, when new immigration laws allowed many more Koreans into the United States. Many Korean immigrants were looking for jobs and better pay in the United States.

Some immigrants also came because they did not enjoy the same freedoms as Americans even in South Korea. Since the South Korean government became more democratic in the late 1980s, fewer South Koreans have moved to the United States.

Most Koreans came from the three largest South Korean cities, including Seoul, the capital. Many Koreans arrived on the West Coast in California, Washington, or Oregon, and most are still there. Besides western cities such as Los Angeles, Korean Americans also traveled east to cities such as New York and Chicago. Many Korean Americans run their own small businesses, both in and outside of cities.

Koreans prize music, sports, and holidays. Music is performed at religious services and ceremonies, as well as enjoyed at work and for pleasure. Classical Korean music uses unique instruments, such as a 12-string zither, and is still enjoyed today. Favorite sports include soccer, archery, and **tae kwon do**, a self-defense martial art.

As in many Asian countries, rice is the most important food in the Korean diet. Korea is well known for a very popular food called **kimchi**. There are many kinds of kimchi, but it is generally made with cabbages,

radishes, Korean red pepper, garlic, salt, and other spices. Kimchi is fermented, which is a process like pickling. Other Korean foods are often highly seasoned, using spicy ingredients such as garlic, ginger, soy sauce, red or black pepper, scallions, and mustard. Common vegetables in Korean cooking include mushrooms, bean sprouts, spinach, carrots, and radishes. Salads usually include cooked ingredients, can be quite spicy, and are eaten in small portions with rice.

Pulgoki is a Korean version of barbecued beef. Beef is marinated in soy sauce, garlic, sugar, sesame oil, and other seasonings before being cooked over a fire. Other favorite Korean dishes are grilled fish, steamed short ribs, mixed vegetables on rice, bellflower root salad, and soy paste stew.

Fruits such as pears and strawberries are often eaten for dessert. For holidays, Koreans make small, colorful rice cakes. The cake shape, content, and color vary from region to region.

This Korean American version of barbecued spare ribs adds a fiery flare to the ribs and is hot . . . hot . . . hot! Instead of barbecuing these ribs over charcoal or flames, this recipe uses the broiler.

Time

15 minutes to prepare
plus
2 hours to marinate
plus
15 minutes to broil

Tools

measuring cups
measuring spoons
1-gallon zipper-lock
plastic bag
small bowl
whisk
cutting board
chef's knife
broiler pan
aluminum foil
oven mitts
tongs
platter

Makes

6 servings

Ingredients

3 to 4 pounds of beef short ribs, separated

½ teaspoon salt

½ teaspoon pepper

⅔ cup teriyaki sauce

1 tablespoon sesame seeds

1 teaspoon sugar

2 teaspoons Tabasco sauce

2 garlic cloves

vegetable oil cooking spray

Steps

1. Sprinkle the short ribs with salt and pepper. Place in a 1-gallon zipper-lock plastic bag.

2. In a small bowl, whisk together the teriyaki sauce, sesame seeds, sugar, and Tabasco sauce. Pour into the plastic bag over the ribs.

3. Place the garlic cloves on a cutting board. Use the side of a large chef's knife to press down on the garlic cloves and loosen the papery skin. Remove the garlic from the skin and add to the plastic bag with the ribs.

4. Seal the zipper-lock bag and let sit in the refrigerator to marinate for 2 hours.

5. Line a broiler pan with aluminum foil. Spray lightly with vegetable oil cooking spray.

6. Set the rack so that the meat will be at least 4 inches from the heat source to avoid burning.

7. Preheat the broiler.

8. Place the spare ribs on the broiler pan. Using oven mitts, place the pan under the broiler. Broil for 7 minutes, watching closely.

9. Take the pan out of the oven and use tongs to turn over the ribs.

10. Place the pan back in the oven and broil for 7 to 8 more minutes. Watch closely. Wash the tongs.

11. Remove the pan from the oven with oven mitts. Use tongs to put the ribs on a serving platter.

Korean Sweet Rice Cakes

Time

Soaking overnight
plus
45 minutes to prepare
plus
2 hours to cool

Tools

cookie sheet
measuring cups
measuring spoons
medium bowl
strainer
medium pot
potato masher
small pot
wooden spoon
plastic wrap
plate

Makes

About 8 rice cakes

More than just another way of using rice, these cakes have a long history in South Korea. They have found their way into many different traditions. This type of rice cake is commonly used for weddings. The cake shape, content, and color vary from one region to another.

Ingredients

vegetable oil for cookie sheet

2 cups sweet rice (also called sticky or glutinous rice)

1 tablespoon soy sauce

⅓ cup brown sugar

¾ cup chestnuts or walnuts, chopped

¾ cup raisins

2 tablespoons pine nuts

2 teaspoons cinnamon

1 tablespoon vegetable oil

Steps

1. Soak the rice in 1 quart of cold water in a medium bowl overnight.

2. Oil a cookie sheet.

3. Drain the water from the rice using a strainer.

4. Place the rice in a medium pot with 2 cups of water. Place on the stove on high and bring the water to a boil. Then cover and reduce the heat to low.

5. Let the rice simmer until the water has evaporated, about 15 minutes. Remove from the heat.

6. Use a potato masher to mash the rice well. Set aside.

7. Place the soy sauce and the brown sugar in a small pot. Heat on medium until it becomes thick in consistency, about 10 minutes. Stir frequently with a wooden spoon.

8. Add the brown sugar mixture to the rice and stir. Add the chestnuts or walnuts, raisins, pine nuts, and cinnamon to the rice and stir again.

9. Spoon the rice mixture onto the oiled cookie sheet.

10. With oiled hands, spread the mixture about ¾ inch thick. Cover loosely with plastic wrap and place in the refrigerator.

11. Once thoroughly cooled, about 2 hours, cut into 1 × 1½-inch rectangles, making sure to oil the knife.

12. Arrange nicely on a plate and serve.

Amazing Asian Dumpling Soup

Wonton wrappers make a sturdy dumpling and are easy to use. Korean American families often make this soup.

Time
45 minutes

Tools
measuring cups
measuring spoons
medium frying pan
colander
medium bowl
paper towels
cutting board
paring knife
grater
waxed paper
small bowl
table fork
wooden spoon
large frying pan or Dutch oven
teaspoon
small bowl
pastry brush
slotted spoon
ladle
8 soup bowls

Makes
8 servings

Ingredients

2 tablespoons peanut oil
½ pound lean ground beef or turkey
2 cups bean sprouts
6 scallions
3 carrots
1 egg
1 tablespoon sesame seeds

½ teaspoon garlic powder
½ teaspoon salt
¼ teaspoon pepper
8 cups low-sodium beef broth
1 cup water
2 tablespoons light soy sauce
1 package wonton wrappers

Steps

1. To make the filling for the dumplings, heat the peanut oil in a medium frying pan over medium heat. Add the ground meat and cook until it is browned. Place the meat into a colander to drain the fat.

2. Put the cooked meat into a medium bowl.

3. Wash the bean sprouts, scallions, and carrots and pat dry with paper towels.

4. On a cutting board, chop the bean sprouts into tiny pieces.

5. Cut the roots off the scallions. Slice the scallions into ¼-inch slices. Slice only the lower third of the green tops.

6. Cut off the carrot tops. Grate the carrots with a metal grater over waxed paper.

7. In a small bowl, beat the egg with a fork.

8. Add the bean sprouts, scallions, carrots, egg, sesame seeds, garlic powder, salt, and pepper to the meat mixture. Mix with a wooden spoon.

9. Place the beef broth, water, and soy sauce in a large frying pan or Dutch oven without the cover. Bring to a boil.

10. Meanwhile, make the dumplings by putting a heaping teaspoon of the filling into the center of each wonton square.

11. Fill a small bowl with water.

12. Brush the edges of the wontons with water. Fold each wonton in half to form a triangle. Press down to make sure the edges are secure. Continue to make dumplings.

13. With a slotted spoon, drop the dumplings into the boiling broth and simmer on medium heat for 10 minutes, being careful that the dumplings do not touch each other.

14. Ladle the soup into soup bowls and serve immediately.

 THAILAND

Thailand is a country in southeastern Asia that is shaped like the head of an elephant with its trunk hanging down. Four countries border Thailand: Myanmar, Laos, Cambodia, and Malaysia. In the middle of the country is a broad plain that is farmed. So much rice is grown here that it is called the "Rice Bowl of Asia." Thailand's climate is tropical, meaning that it is hot and humid most of the time.

Immigrants from Thailand are mostly recent arrivals, coming after 1960. Thai immigrants include many professional people, such as doctors and engineers. Many left Thailand because of problems finding jobs in their fields. Some felt threatened by wars going on in neighboring countries, such as Laos and Cambodia. Thai immigrants have settled mainly in California, Washington, Illinois, Texas, Florida, and New York.

The Thai people have brought many traditions to the United States, including dancing, theater, music, games, and their own version of boxing. There are about 50 types of Thai musical instruments. Thai boxers not only use their hands when they box but can use their knees, feet, and elbows. Soccer is also a popular sport.

Thais have brought their cooking traditions with them as well.

- In the center of the table at every meal (even breakfast) is white rice, and it is surrounded by any number of main dishes, such as shrimp with sweet chile sauce or red curry beef. Rice helps to soak up liquids and also takes away some of the heat from hot, spicy foods. Jasmine rice is especially popular because of its nutty, toasty flavor.

- Each dish is carefully arranged and decorated to look delicious. Fruits and vegetables, such as mangoes and carrots, are often carefully cut into shapes, such as a flower, to make a dish look even more appealing.

- Thai food could never be called bland! Thai cooks use lots of herbs, spices, and sometimes hot chile peppers. **Fish sauce**, a salty brown sauce, is essential to Thai cooking. It is important for each dish to be balanced, meaning that there is a balance of salty, sour, hot, and sweet ingredients.

- The typical sweet in Thailand is fruit. Due to the country's tropical climate, Thai meals usually include fruit such as bananas, melons of all sorts, pineapple, mangoes, and papayas.

Favorite dishes include soups, salads, stir-fries, noodle dishes, and curries. Soups may be very simple, such as lemongrass soup. Lemongrass is a tall grass, and the lower part of it is used to give soup and many other foods a lemony flavor. Soups may also include other ingredients, such as chicken or fish, noodles or rice, and vegetables.

Salads are very popular, in part because many vegetables are grown in Thailand and also because cool salads taste great in the hot weather. Cucumber salad with vinegar dressing is a favorite.

Thai noodles are made with rice flour or mung beans and sometimes colored with vegetables. A favorite Thai dish made in the United States is **pad thai**, which is rice noodles tossed with chicken or shrimp, peanuts, bean sprouts, and tofu.

Thai curries are prepared with a spicy paste made from fresh ingredients such as lemongrass and chiles. Curry dishes are like stews and are most often made with meat or chicken and vegetables. Thai curries can be quite hot due to the use of fiery chile peppers. Coconut milk is sometimes used to tame hot chiles and mellow flavors.

Time
15 minutes

Tools
cutting board
paring knife
measuring cups
measuring spoons
medium bowl
whisk
paper towels
4 plates
serving spoon

Makes
4 servings

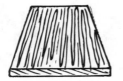

Thai chicken salad is typical of Thai dishes because it includes a balance of sweet, sour, hot, and salty tastes, and you can adjust the flavors as you like. There are many versions of this Thai-created dish in America.

Ingredients

1   lime

¼ cup peanut oil

1   tablespoon fish sauce (available in some supermarkets or in Asian grocery stores)

⅛ teaspoon crushed red pepper

3   scallions

8   romaine leaves

1   teaspoon brown sugar

2   cups bite-sized pieces cooked chicken

2   tablespoons chopped peanuts

Steps

1. On a cutting board, cut the lime in half. Squeeze the lime to make 2 tablespoons of fresh lime juice. Place the lime juice in a medium bowl.

2. To make the dressing, add the peanut oil, fish sauce, and crushed red pepper to the medium bowl. Use a whisk to blend the ingredients.

3. Wash the scallions and romaine leaves and pat dry with paper towels. Cut off the roots of the scallions. Chop the white part only and add to the bowl.

4. Place the romaine leaves on 4 plates.

5. Taste the dressing. Add about 1 teaspoon of brown sugar as needed to balance the flavors in the way you like best.

6. Add the chicken to the dressing and toss to coat well.

7. Place the chicken salad on top of the lettuce leaves on the plates. Garnish with chopped peanuts.

Sticky Rice with Fruit

Sticky rice is a sweet rice that sticks together. It makes a great Thai dessert when mixed with coconut milk and served with fruit, such as mango or papaya.

Ingredients

1 cup sweet rice (also called sticky or glutinous rice)

1 quart water

2 cups water

1 cup canned coconut milk

⅓ cup sugar

¼ teaspoon salt

2 cups sliced fresh fruit such as mangoes, papayas, or bananas

¼ cup coconut cream (the thick part of coconut milk)

Steps

1. Soak the rice in 1 quart of water in a medium bowl for 1 hour.

2. Place the rice in a strainer. Rinse the rice under cold running water until the water draining away looks clear.

3. Place the rice in a medium saucepan with 2 cups of water.

4. Put the heat on high and bring the water to a boil. Then cover and reduce the heat to low so that the rice simmers.

5. Cook the rice until the water has evaporated, about 10 to 15 minutes.

6. While the rice simmers, combine the coconut milk, sugar, and salt in a small saucepan. Place over medium heat and cook for 3 to 4 minutes, stirring constantly with a wooden spoon. Do not boil.

7. Pour the coconut milk mixture over the cooked rice in the medium saucepan. Toss well so that the rice is coated. Cover and let it sit for 30 minutes.

Time
1 hour to soak rice
plus
45 minutes to cook

Tools
measuring cups
measuring spoons
medium bowl
strainer
medium saucepan with lid
can opener
small saucepan
wooden spoon
paring knife
cutting board
4 dessert plates
scoop

Makes
4 servings

8. While the rice sits, peel and slice the fruit on a cutting board. Divide the fruit up among 4 dessert plates.

9. Scoop the rice and divide among the plates. Drizzle 1 tablespoon of coconut cream (the thick part of coconut milk) over each rice scoop. Serve.

CHAPTER 18

TURKEY

Turkey is unique because it has a foothold in two continents: Asia and Europe. Most of Turkey is in Asia, but the northwest corner is actually in Europe. Water separates the Asian part of Turkey from the European part. Turkey is surrounded by the Black Sea to the north, the Aegean Sea to the west, and the Mediterranean Sea to the south. The geography is quite wide-ranging, with long coastlines, fertile grasslands, mountain ranges, plains, and plateaus. The climate varies too. Along the coasts, warm weather and fertile soil allow farmers to grow wheat, oats, barley, lentils, almonds, figs, apricots, chickpeas, and olives.

Turkey was the center of the Ottoman Empire for over 600 years since the 1300s. The Ottoman Empire was a powerful civilization founded by the Ottoman Turks, who spread their Muslim religion as they conquered parts of Asia, Europe, the Middle East, and northern Africa. In decline for many years, this empire was defeated in World War I (1914–1918). In 1923, the Republic of Turkey was born.

Most of the Turks who immigrated to the United States came during the 1900s. Turks who entered the United States from 1900 to 1921 left the Ottoman Empire to earn money, and most settled in and around major cities such as New York, Boston, Chicago, Detroit, and San Francisco. Some returned to Turkey with their earnings. During the 1950s, bad economic times and restricted human rights pushed some Turks to come to the United States. Larger numbers arrived after 1965, when America's immigration laws changed. They settled in states such as New York, California, Florida, and Michigan.

Turkish culture includes exciting music, dance, art, and theater of all kinds. Folk and pop music are popular. Styles of dancing include everything from ballet to belly dancing. Turkey is well known for its beautiful carpets made in bright colors with striking patterns.

Turkish culture also includes a wonderful cooking tradition. Lamb, rice, yogurt, olive oil, eggplant, and bread are common foods and ingredients. Lamb is the most popular meat in Turkey. Because many Turks are Muslim, they cannot eat pork. Seafood is also popular. Many vegetables are grown, including eggplant, which is served in over 40 different ways!

Turkish foods that we enjoy in America include **kebabs**, which are grilled and seasoned meat and vegetables, such as grilled lamb with peppers, tomatoes, and eggplant. Sometimes the kebabs are placed on skewers (like big metal toothpicks) for cooking over a fire. The meat and vegetables are then served on a flat, oval-shaped bread, called **pide**.

Dinner usually starts with appetizers, called **mezzes**, laid out on a table. Favorite mezzes include vegetables that are served cold or at room temperature, such as roasted eggplant and hot pepper salad. Other mezzes may use ingredients such as grilled lamb, chicken, or seafood. Mezzes are very small and can be eaten in one or two bites at most.

The main course may include dishes such as lemon chicken with okra, stuffed mackerel, grilled lamb, manti, or dolma. **Manti** is a small pasta filled with a special meat mixture and served with a yogurt-garlic sauce.

Dolmas are vegetables stuffed with spiced rice, vegetables, and/or meat. Salads and pilafs are common side dishes. **Pilaf** is a rice dish made with ingredients such as almonds, meat, raisins, and black olives.

Dessert is often fruit, pudding such as rice pudding, or sweet pastries such as baklava. **Baklava** is made with layers of paper-thin pastry filled with chopped nuts and drizzled with a rich honey-based syrup. It is cut into diamond-shaped pieces before it is served.

Bob's Scrambled Eggs (Menemen)

Time
20 minutes

Tools
cutting board
paring knife
small frying pan
measuring cups
measuring spoons
wooden spoon
medium bowl
table fork
whisk
large nonstick frying pan
rubber spatula

Makes
4 to 6 servings

Bob is a Turkish American we know who remembers waking up to the smell of this spicy vegetable and egg dish when he was growing up. Try it for breakfast along with juice and rolls.

Ingredients

1   small onion
1   tablespoon margarine
8   eggs
⅛   teaspoon ground red pepper
½   teaspoon salt

¼   teaspoon pepper
½   teaspoon paprika
    vegetable oil cooking spray
1   cup diced tomatoes

Steps

1. Remove the papery skin from the onion. On a cutting board, cut the onion in half. With the flat sides down, cut each onion half into pieces.

2. Preheat a small frying pan on medium heat for 2 minutes. Add the margarine and melt.

3. Use a wooden spoon to cook the onion in the frying pan for about 3 minutes or until tender. Turn off the heat and set aside.

4. Break the eggs into a medium bowl and beat with a fork.

5. Add the red pepper, salt, black pepper, and paprika to the eggs. Whisk vigorously for 1 minute until the eggs are fluffy.

6. Spray a large nonstick frying pan with vegetable oil cooking spray. Preheat the pan on medium heat for 2 minutes.

7. Add the onions and tomatoes evenly in the pan. Pour the egg mixture over the onions and tomatoes. Adjust the heat to medium-low.

8. Gently scramble the egg mixture for about 5 minutes with a rubber spatula until set.

9. Serve with rolls or crusty bread for a satisfying breakfast.

···· Overstuffed ···· Zucchini

Time

30 minutes to prepare
plus
30 minutes to bake

Tools

paper towels
cutting board
paring knife
teaspoon
small frying pan
measuring cups
measuring spoons
wooden spoon
medium bowl
whisk
cookie sheet
oven mitts
spatula

Makes

4 to 6 servings

Stuffing vegetables, such as eggplants, peppers, yellow squash, and zucchini, with cheeses, bread crumbs, eggs, herbs, and spices has been a Turkish cooking tradition for centuries.

Ingredients

4 medium zucchini	½ cup crumbled feta cheese
1 medium onion	¾ cup grated Swiss cheese
1 garlic clove	1 tablespoon dried parsley
1 tablespoon margarine	1 teaspoon dried dill
½ teaspoon salt	2 tablespoons all-purpose flour
½ teaspoon pepper	vegetable oil cooking spray
3 eggs	1 teaspoon paprika

Steps

1. Wash the zucchini and dry with paper towels. On a cutting board, cut the zucchini lengthwise.

2. Scoop out the insides of the zucchini with a teaspoon, leaving a ½-inch rim around the edge.

3. Chop the scooped-out zucchini into small pieces.

4. Remove the papery skin from the onion. On a cutting board, cut the onion in half. With the flat sides down, cut each onion half into small pieces.

5. Peel the papery skin off the garlic clove. Cut the garlic clove into slices and finely mince.

6. Preheat a small frying pan over medium heat for 1 minute. Add the margarine.

7. When the margarine is melted, add the onion and garlic. Use a wooden spoon and cook for 2 minutes.

8. Add the chopped zucchini, salt, and pepper. Cook for about 5 minutes or until all of the vegetables are tender.

9. Break the eggs into a medium bowl. Whisk the eggs vigorously until fluffy, about 1 minute.

10. Stir the cooked vegetable mixture, feta cheese, Swiss cheese, parsley, dill, and flour into the beaten eggs. Stir well with a wooden spoon.

11. Preheat the oven to 375°F.

12. Spray a cookie sheet lightly with vegetable oil cooking spray.

13. Put the zucchini halves on the cookie sheet and fill with the vegetable and cheese mixture. Dust the tops lightly with paprika.

14. Use oven mitts to put the cookie sheet in the oven. Bake for 30 minutes or until the filling is set.

15. Using oven mitts, remove the tray from the oven. Allow to cool for 5 minutes before using a spatula to serve.

···· The Best Baklava ····

Time
30 minutes to prepare
plus
40 minutes to bake

Tools
measuring cups
measuring spoons
large zipper-lock plastic
bag
rolling pin
small bowl
wooden spoon
microwave-safe dish with
lid
cookie sheet with sides
waxed paper
kitchen towel
pastry brush
paring knife
large pot
oven mitts

Makes
2 dozen squares

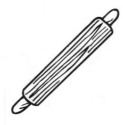

Baklava is Turkey's most famous dessert. It is made with layers of paper-thin pastry dough filled with chopped nuts and drizzled with a rich honey-based syrup.

Ingredients

1 cup walnuts
1 cup pecans
½ cup sugar
1 teaspoon cinnamon
¼ teaspoon ground cloves
8 tablespoons margarine
(1 stick)
vegetable oil cooking spray

1 small box prepared phyllo
pastry dough, thawed in
refrigerator

The Sweetest Syrup
2 cups sugar
1 cup honey
1 teaspoon lemon extract
2 cups water

Steps

1. Place the walnuts and pecans in a large zipper-lock plastic bag. Press out the air and zip tight. With a rolling pin, roll back and forth over the nuts to break them into small pieces.

2. Place the nuts in a small bowl, and add the sugar, cinnamon, and cloves. Mix together with a wooden spoon.

3. Place the margarine in a microwave-safe dish with a lid. Microwave on high power for about 30 seconds or until liquid.

4. Spray a cookie sheet with 1-inch sides with vegetable oil cooking spray.

5. Remove the phyllo from its plastic bag. Lay flat and cover with waxed paper weighted down with a damp towel.

6. Using a pastry brush, lightly brush 6 sheets of phyllo pastry dough with margarine.

7. Layer the sheets on top of one another on the cookie sheet, then sprinkle top with ¼ of the nut mixture.

8. Repeat steps 6 and 7 three more times, using a total of 24 sheets of phyllo and ending with the nut mixture on top.

9. Preheat the oven to 350°F.

10. With a paring knife, cut the phyllo in diamond shapes as a decoration. Do not cut the phyllo all the way through.

11. Use oven mitts to place the cookie sheet in the oven. Bake for 40 minutes or until golden brown.

12. While the baklava bakes, prepare the syrup. In a large pot, bring the sugar, honey, lemon extract, and water to a boil. Lower the heat to a simmer. Stir with a wooden spoon on medium-low heat for 10 minutes. Turn off the heat. Let cool for 20 minutes.

13. Remove the baklava from the oven with oven mitts.

14. Pour the syrup over the baklava. Cut into diamond shapes and enjoy.

GLOSSARY

antipasto The first course of an Italian meal in which a small portion of food is served.

arroz con pollo A Spanish dish of chicken with rice.

baba ghanoush Eggplant dip, a Middle Eastern dish.

babka A cake that originated in eastern Europe and was brought to New York by Polish immigrants.

baklava A famous Turkish dessert made with layers of paper-thin pastry filled with chopped nuts and drizzled with a rich honey-based syrup.

batidos Icy Cuban drinks.

biscotti An Italian cookie that is baked twice.

bok choy A vegetable popular in Chinese cooking that has long white stalks and green leaves. Also called Chinese cabbage.

boli A West African dish of baked plantains.

boniato Sweet potatoes eaten in Cuba that taste a bit like chestnuts.

bossa nova A popular Brazilian music that combines jazz with unique rhythms.

boxty A type of potato bread from Ireland that is baked or fried on a griddle like pancakes.

bratwurst A German sausage made with pork and spices that is common in the United States.

bulgur Wheat kernels that have been steamed, dried, and crushed. Commonly used in Middle Eastern cooking.

burritos A soft flour tortilla that is usually filled with beans and meat, then rolled up. A Mexican dish, burritos are often served with lettuce, tomatoes, salsa, and sour cream.

cannoli An Italian cream-filled pastry.

cappuccino A hot beverage made with espresso coffee and hot milk.

chicharrones de pollo A Cuban dish in which small pieces of chicken are marinated in lime juice and soy sauce, then breaded and fried.

chimichanga A fried burrito.

churrasco A Brazilian dish in which meats are put on a skewer, grilled, and served.

chutney An Indian relish made from fruits and/or vegetables, and herbs and spices.

couscous A pasta popular in North Africa that's made from semolina. Also refers to a North African dish in which couscous is topped with a stew that is spicy but not hot.

curry A spicy Indian stew.

dal A creamy vegetarian dish made in India of legumes with vegetables, garlic, and spices.

dodo A West African dish of fried plantains.

dolmas In Turkey, vegetables, such as grape leaves or green peppers, stuffed with spiced rice, vegetables, and/or meat.

dubke Lebanese national dance.

Dublin coddle An Irish stew of potatoes, bacon, and ham.

duck sauce Also called plum sauce, a sauce in Chinese cooking made from plums, apricots, and other ingredients, popular as a dipping sauce.

enchilada A Mexican rolled-up tortilla stuffed with fillings and baked with sauce and cheese.

fajita A Mexican dish with grilled meat and possibly grilled vegetables such as green peppers served on a flour tortilla with condiments such as lettuce, tomatoes, sour cream, and salsa.

feijoada   Brazil's national dish consisting of a stew of beef, pork, sausage, and black beans.

fish sauce   A salty brown sauce essential to cooking in Thailand.

fjord   A part of the sea that goes inland from the coast and has steep slopes going up from the water. Common in the Scandinavian countries.

flan   A baked custard with caramel topping.

fufu   A starchy accompaniment to stews and other dishes with sauces in Nigeria. Traditional fufu is made with pounded yams or plantains.

futebol   Spanish for soccer.

guava   A pale green pear-shaped tropical fruit that is only 2 to 3 inches long.

hearts of palm   The edible inner portion of the stem of the cabbage palm tree, which grows in many tropical climates such as Brazil.

hoisin sauce   A dark, sweet sauce made from soybeans, sugar, and spices that is used in Chinese cooking.

hummus   A chickpea and sesame spread popular in Middle Eastern cooking.

injera   A flat, spongy bread made in Ethiopia from teff flour.

Irish soda bread   An Irish bread in which a chemical reaction between the baking soda and buttermilk or sour milk causes the bread to rise. This is how the bread got its name.

Irish stew   A stew from Ireland made with lamb, potatoes, onions, carrots, and sometimes other vegetables.

jalisco   A Mexican folk dance that dates back to the 1700s and is used when a man is dating a woman.

jicama   A brown root vegetable with white flesh that is tasty in salads. It is popular in Mexican cooking.

jollof rice   A typical Nigerian main dish that combines vegetables, a starch such as rice, and meat or fish (if available) into a one-pot meal.

kebab   Grilled and seasoned meat and vegetables sometimes served on a skewer or on bread. A popular dish in Turkey and other Arab countries.

khubz   A Moroccan flat bread.

kibbeh   A Lebanese dish of ground lamb mixed with spices and bulgur and baked in a flat pan.

kimchi   A favorite Korean food made with cabbage, radish, Korean red pepper, garlic, salt, and other spices. Kimchi is fermented to give it a unique taste.

kulfi   An Indian version of ice cream flavored with pistachio, mango, or other flavors.

kumquat   A small fruit popular in Chinese cooking that resembles an orange but is not a citrus fruit.

litchis   A round, red fruit that tastes like raisins and is popular in Chinese cooking.

lo mein   A Chinese dish of boiled noodles combined with various stir-fried ingredients, such as chicken and vegetables. The cooked noodles and the stir-fried ingredients are tossed at the last minute with the stir-fry sauce just enough to heat and coat all of the ingredients.

malanga   A vegetable popular in Cuba that is similar to a yam and is often made into chips and used in soups and stews.

manioc   A vegetable in Brazil that is used to make flour and is boiled and eaten like potatoes, also called *cassava*.

manti   A small pasta filled with a special meat mixture and served with a yogurt-garlic sauce.

mariachi   A traditional form of Mexican music that blends the sounds of brass and string instruments.

masala   A blend of herbs and spices used in Indian cooking.

mazur   A traditional Polish folk dance.

mezze   Arabic word meaning "appetizers." Very small portions of food.

mishwi   A popular Lebanese dish of meat kebabs often served with rice.

mojo   A sauce of garlic, citrus juice, oil, and fresh herbs that is added to food at the table.

moros y cristianos   A Cuban dish meaning "Moors and Christians" that includes white rice, black beans, onions, garlic, green peppers, and tomatoes.

oud   A pear-shaped instrument played like a guitar in Lebanon.

oyster sauce   Used in Chinese cooking, a thick brown sauce that has a sweet, smoky flavor.

pad thai   A Thai dish of rice noodles tossed with chicken, shrimp, peanuts, bean sprouts, and tofu.

parantha   An Indian whole-wheat flat bread.

picadillo   A Cuban dish with ground beef that is flavored with olives, raisins, tomatoes, peppers, and onions and served with rice.

pide   A flat, oval Turkish bread served plain or filled with meat.

pierogies   A Polish food similar to ravioli that is filled with meat, cheese, sauerkraut, mushrooms, or other fillings.

pilaf   A rice dish with almonds, meat, raisins, and black olives.

plantain   Large banana that must be cooked before eating.

plum sauce   Also called duck sauce, a sauce in Chinese cooking made from plums, apricots, and other ingredients; popular as a dipping sauce.

polenta   Cornmeal porridge from Italy.

pulgoki   A Korean version of barbecued beef.

quesadillas   A Mexican dish like a grilled cheese sandwich that uses a tortilla for the bread.

quindim   A Brazilian upside-down dessert made with eggs, sugar, and grated coconut.

raita   An Indian dish of grated raw vegetables mixed with yogurt, like a salad.

risotto   A creamy rice dish served with grated cheese from Italy.

ropa vieja   A Cuban dish of spicy shredded strips of beef with vegetables.

rosemaling   Decorative folk painting of Norway that involves painting flowers on wooden home furnishings, such as tables, chairs, and trunks.

rumba   An Afro-Cuban dance style based on drum rhythms.

samba   A famous Brazilian dance with African origins.

sauerbraten   A German dish of marinated roast beef.

smorgasbord   A Scandinavian buffet of many dishes from which guests can taste a little of many foods.

son   The native dance music of Cuba.

tabbouleh   A popular Middle Eastern salad featuring bulgur and vegetables.

taco   A Mexican food of meat and beans stuffed in a folded tortilla and garnished with salsa and chopped lettuce.

tae kwon do   A self-defense martial art popular in Korea.

tahini   Sesame seed paste used to make hummus.

tajine   A Moroccan stew of meat and vegetables, sometimes with the addition of fruits and nuts. A typical tajine might include lamb with dates.

tandoori   A meat or chicken dish that is first marinated in lime juice, oil, and yogurt. Small chunks of the meat or poultry are then put on skewers and roasted in a clay oven called a *tandoor*.

wat   A peppery stew made in Ethiopia that is served on injera, a flat bread.

wok   An all-purpose Chinese pan that is used for stir-frying because its even heat allows quick cooking. It looks like a wide cone that is rounded at the bottom.

yucca   A vegetable, also called *cassava*. Popular in Cuban cooking, it is used like a potato.

INDEX

beef (*continued*)
  Korean-Style Short Ribs, 144–145
  See also meats
Beef Stir-Fry with Rice, Sichuan-Style,
    27–28
Berbers, in Morocco, 101–102
Best Baklava, 164–165
beverages
  Banana Milkshake, 106
  Banana Strawberry Batidos, 36
  coffee, 16–17, 40
  in Italian cuisine, 77
  in Moroccan cuisine, 102, 106–107
  tea, 24, 40, 102, 107
Black Forest Cherry Torte, 48
Bob's Scrambled Eggs (Menemen),
    160–161
boli, in Nigerian cuisine, 118
boniato, in Cuban cuisine, 33
Boxty, in Irish cuisine, 67
Bratwurst with Sauerkraut, 49
Brazil, 15–20
breads
  Ethiopian Injera, 40–42
  of German immigrants, 47
  in Indian cuisine, 57
  Irish Soda Bread, 67–69
  in Moroccan cuisine, 102
  Moroccan Lemon Anise Bread,
    107–108
  Naan, 58–59
  in Norwegian cuisine, 125
  in Polish cuisine, 133
  Shilling Bun, 128–129
  in Turkish cuisine, 158

breakfast foods
  Bob's Scrambled Eggs (Menemen),
    160–161
  Cuban, 34
  Dutch, 110
  in Norwegian cuisine, 125
  Norwegian Waffles, 127
  Sausage Roll, 120–121
  Shilling Bun, 128–129
Britain
  India and, 56
  Ireland and, 66
bulgur, in Lebanese cuisine, 84–85
burritos, 91

Cabbage Rolls, Mildred Goldberg's
    Amazing Stuffed, 134–135
Cabral, Pedro Alvares, 15
carne asada, in Mexican cuisine, 92
cheeses
  in Dutch cuisine, 110
  in Italian cuisine, 76
  in Mexican cuisine, 92
chicharrones de pollo, in Cuban cuisine,
    33
chicken
  Chicken Lo Mein, 25–26
  cleaning up after, 13
  in Cuban cuisine, 33–34
  Curried Chicken, 60–61
  molé, 92
  Thai Chicken Salad, 154
Chicken Lo Mein, 25–26
chile peppers, in Mexican cuisine, 91
China, 21–29

eggs (*continued*)
  separating, 10
Ellis Island, immigration through, 2
enchiladas, 91
England, immigrants from, 1
English, immigrants speaking, 45
equipment, cooking, 4–6
equivalents, 8
Ethiopia, 38–44
Ethiopian Injera, 41–42
Ethiopian Vegetable Bowl, 43–44
Europe, immigrants from, 1–2
Everyday Escarole, Bean, and Barley
  Soup, 78

fajitas, 91
famine, as reason for immigration, 22,
  39, 55, 65–66, 76, 110
feijoada, in Brazilian cuisine, 16
Filomena's Love Knot Cookies, 80–81
flan, in Cuban cuisine, 34
frankfurters, 47
freedom, as reason for immigration, 32,
  45, 124, 132, 142, 158
fruits
  Anytime Apple and Blackberry Pie,
    72–73
  Banana Milkshake, 106
  Banana Strawberry Batidos, 36
  in Brazilian cuisine, 16–17
  in Chinese cuisine, 23–24
  Dutch Apple Cake, 113–114
  Fried Bananas with Cinnamon, 19
  Ginger-Scented Fruits with Orange
    Sorbet, 29

in Indian cuisine, 57
in Korean cuisine, 143
in Lebanese cuisine, 84–85
in Mexican cuisine, 91–92
in Moroccan cuisine, 103
in Nigerian cuisine, 118–119
in Norwegian cuisine, 125
Sticky Rice with Fruit, 155–156
in Thai cuisine, 152
fufu, in Nigerian cuisine, 118

German Potato Salad, 50–51
Germany, 45–53
  immigrants from, 1, 75
germs, 13
Gingerbread People, 52–53
grains
  bulgur in Lebanese cuisine, 84–85,
    87–88
  couscous, 102, 104–105
  in Ethiopian cuisine, 40–41
  in Lebanese cuisine, 84
  in Norwegian cuisine, 125
  in Polish cuisine, 133
guacamole, 93–94
guava, in Cuban cuisine, 34

hearts of palm, in Brazilian cuisine, 17
Hitler, Adolf, 46
holidays
  Korean, 142–143
  Mexican, 90
Holland. *See* Netherlands, the
hummus, 85–86
Hummus Bi-tahini, 86

immigration
  diseases as reason for, 39, 45–46, 76
  famine as reason for, 22, 39, 55,
    65–66, 76, 110
  freedom as reason for, 32, 45, 124,
    132, 142, 158
  laws limiting, 1, 22–23, 55–56, 141,
    158
  motives for, 1, 23, 40, 56, 118, 141
  political unrest as reason for, 22, 46,
    90
  politics as reason for, 32, 124
  poverty as reason for, 16, 22, 65, 76,
    90, 110, 131–132, 158
  religion as reason for, 45, 66, 83–84,
    110, 124
  wars as reason for, 39, 45–46, 83–84,
    117, 151
  waves of, 1–2
India, 55–63
ingredients
  difference of American, 1, 37, 67
  Mexican vs. American, 92
Injera, 40–42
Ireland, 1, 65–73
Irish Soda Bread, Mom's, 67–69
Irish Stew, 67
Italy, 1, 75–81

Jews, immigration by, 46, 132
jobs
  for Chinese immigrants, 22
  for German immigrants, 46
  for Indian immigrants, 55–56
  for Lebanese immigrants, 84

  for Mexican immigrants, 90
  for Polish immigrants, 132
  for Thai immigrants, 151
jollof rice, in Nigerian cuisine, 118

kebabs, in Turkish cuisine, 158
khubz, in Moroccan cuisine, 102
kibbeh, in Lebanese cuisine, 85
kimchi, in Korean cuisine, 142
Korean Sweet Rice Cakes, 146–147
Korean-Style Short Ribs, 144–145

Lebanon, 83–85
legumes, in Indian cuisine, 56
lentils. See beans
literature
  Irish, 66
  Nigerian, 118
  Polish, 132
Lo Mein, Chicken, 25–26

malanga, in Cuban cuisine, 33
manioc, in Brazilian cuisine, 17
manti, in Turkish cuisine, 158
marinades, 47, 144
masala, in Indian cuisine, 56
Mashed Yams, 122
meals, types of dishes served
  in China, 24
  in Italy, 78
  in Thailand, 152
measuring terms, 8
meats
  Bratwurst with Sauerkraut, 49
  in Brazilian cuisine, 16

rice
    Basmati Rice, 62–63
    in Chinese cuisine, 23
    in Cuban cuisine, 33
    in Italian cuisine, 76
    in Korean cuisine, 142–143
    Korean Sweet Rice Cakes, 146–147
    in Nigerian cuisine, 118
    Savory Shrimp Dinner over Rice, 79
    Sticky Rice with Fruit, 155–156
    in Thai cuisine, 152
    in Turkish cuisine, 159
ropa vieja, in Cuban cuisine, 33

safety rules, 11–13
salads
    German Potato Salad, 50–51
    Mexican Bean Salad, 99
    Thai Chicken Salad, 154
    in Thai cuisine, 152
    in Turkish cuisine, 159
salsa
    in Mexican cooking, 91–92
    Oh-So-Hot Salsa, 95–96
sandwiches
    Cuban, 34–35
    in Norwegian cuisine, 125
    Open-Faced Roast Beef Sandwich, 126
sauces
    in Chinese cooking, 24
    in Cuban cooking, 33
    in Mexican cooking, 91–92, 95–96
    Oh-So-Hot Salsa, 95–96
    in Thai cooking, 152
sauerbraten, 47

sauerkraut, 47
Sauerkraut, Bratwurst with, 49
Sausage Roll, 120–121
sausages
    of German immigrants, 47, 49
    in Italian cuisine, 76
    in Polish cuisine, 132
    Sausage Roll, 120–121
Savory Shrimp Dinner over Rice, 79
Scotland, immigrants from, 1
seafood
    cleaning up after, 13
    in Italian cuisine, 76
    in Lebanese cuisine, 84
    in Norwegian cuisine, 124
    in Turkish cuisine, 158
    Savory Shrimp Dinner over Rice, 79
Shilling Bun, 128–129
Sichuan-Style Beef Stir-Fry with Rice,
    27–28
skills, cooking, 7–10
slavery, 117–118
    in Brazil, 16
    in Cuba, 32
smorgasbord, in Norwegian cuisine, 125
snacks
    in German cuisine, 47
    in Lebanese cuisine, 85
    in Nigerian cuisine, 118–119
    Sausage Roll, 120–121
sofrito, in Cuban cuisine, 33
soups
    Amazing Asian Dumpling Soup,
    148–149
    in Chinese cuisine, 24